"A SHARPLY OBSERVED, HILARIOUS COMEDY, SEAMLESSLY WOVEN INTO THE STUFF OF THE HUMAN SPIRIT." —Dennis Cunningham, WCBS-TV

"Honest . . . a skillful mixture of comedy and drama . . . as funny as anything Mr. Simon has written."
                                    —*Wall Street Journal*

"Funny, affectionate, and . . . perceptive."
                                    —*Christian Science Monitor*

"A REAL TREAT . . . an event of note."
                                    —*Chattanooga Times*

"True, poignant, and gentle, with . . . some of Simon's funniest lines."   —*Women's Wear Daily*

"PERFECT . . . a poignant slice of life with an . . . abundance of dramatic and humorous incidents . . . keen dialogue . . . a pleasure to read."   —*Booklist*

Since 1960 a Broadway season without a NEIL SIMON comedy or musical has been a rare one. He is the winner of three Tony Awards for Best Play (*The Odd Couple*, *Biloxi Blues*, and *Lost in Yonkers*) and the 1991 Pulitzer Prize for Drama for *Lost in Yonkers*. Mr. Simon's most recent plays are *Jake's Women*, *Laughter on the 23rd Floor*, and *London Suite*. He lives in California.

BRIGHTON BEACH MEMOIRS

NEIL SIMON

A PLUME BOOK

PLUME
Published by the Penguin Group
Penguin Books USA Inc., 375 Hudson Street,
New York, New York 10014, U.S.A.
Penguin Books Ltd, 27 Wrights Lane, London W8 5TZ, England
Penguin Books Australia Ltd, Ringwood, Victoria, Australia
Penguin Books Canada Ltd, 10 Alcorn Avenue,
Toronto, Ontario, Canada M4V 3B2
Penguin Books (N.Z.) Ltd, 182–190 Wairau Road,
Auckland 10, New Zealand

Penguin Books Ltd, Registered Offices:
Harmondsworth, Middlesex, England

Published by Plume, an imprint of Dutton Signet, a division of Penguin
Books USA Inc. Published by arrangement with Random House, Inc. For
information address Random House, Inc., 201 W. 50th Street, New York,
NY 10022. Previously appeared in a Signet edition.

First Plume Printing, November, 1995
10 9 8 7 6

℗ REGISTERED TRADEMARK—MARCA REGISTRADA
LIBRARY OF CONGRESS CATALOGING-IN-PUBLICATION DATA
Simon, Neil.
    Brighton Beach memoirs / Neil Simon.
        p.   cm.
    Previously published: Signet, 1984.
    ISBN 0-452-27528-8
    I. Title.
PS3537.I663B7   1995
812'.54—dc20   95–21788
                                            CIP
Printed in the United States of America

To my parents, grandparents, brother,
cousins, aunts, uncles, and especially to those who
endured the pains, insecurities, fears, joys,
love and fellowship of New York City
in the Depression Years

BRIGHTON BEACH MEMOIRS *was first presented on December 10, 1982, at the Ahmanson Theatre, Los Angeles, and on March 27, 1983, at the Alvin Theatre, New York City, with the following cast:*

EUGENE	Matthew Broderick
BLANCHE	Joyce Van Patten
KATE	Elizabeth Franz
LAURIE	Mandy Ingber
NORA	Jodi Thelen
STANLEY	Željko Ivanek
JACK	Peter Michael Goetz

Directed by Gene Saks
Setting by David Mitchell
Lighting by Tharon Musser
Costumes by Patricia Zipprodt

SYNOPSIS OF SCENES

ACT ONE

Brighton Beach, Brooklyn, New York
September 1937—6:30 P.M.

ACT TWO

Wednesday, a week later
About 6:30 in the evening

ACT ONE

Brighton Beach, New York. September 1937. A wooden frame house, not too far from the beach. It is a lower-middle-income area inhabited mostly by Jews, Irish and Germans.

The entrance to the house is to the right: a small porch and two steps up that lead to the front door. Inside we see the dining room and living-room area. Another door leads to the kitchen . . . A flight of stairs leads up to three small bedrooms. Unseen are two other bedrooms. A hallway leads to other rooms . . .

It's around six-thirty and the late-September sun is sinking fast. KATE JEROME, *about forty years old, is setting the table. Her sister,* BLANCHE MORTON, *thirty-eight, is working at a sewing machine.* LAURIE MORTON, *aged thirteen, is lying on the sofa reading a book.*

Outside on the grass stands EUGENE JEROME, *almost but not quite fifteen. He is wearing knickers, a shirt and tie, a faded and torn sweater, Keds sneakers and a blue baseball cap. He has a beaten and worn baseball glove on his left hand, and in his right hand he holds a softball that is so old and battered that it is ready to fall apart.*

On an imaginary pitcher's mound, facing left, he looks back over his shoulder to an imaginary runner on second, then back over to the "batter." Then he winds up and pitches, hitting an offstage wall.

EUGENE One out, a man on second, bottom of the seventh, two balls, no strikes . . . Ruffing checks the runner on second, gets the sign from Dickey, Ruffing stretches, Ruffing pitches—*(He throws the ball)* Caught the inside corner, steerike one! Atta baby! No hitter up there. *(He retrieves the ball)* One out, a man on second, bottom of the seventh, two balls, one strike . . . Ruffing checks the runner on second, gets the sign from

Dickey, Ruffing stretches, Ruffing pitches—*(He throws the ball)* Low and outside, ball three. Come on, Red! Make him a hitter! No batter up there. In there all the time, Red.

BLANCHE *(Stops sewing)* Kate, please. My head is splitting.

KATE I told that boy a hundred and nine times. *(She yells out)* Eugene! Stop banging the wall!

EUGENE *(Calls out)* In a minute, Ma! This is for the World Series! *(Back to his game)* One out, a man on second, bottom of the seventh, three balls, one strike . . . Ruffing stretches, Ruffing pitches—*(He throws the ball)* Oh, no! High and outside, JoJo Moore walks! First and second and Mel Ott lopes up to the plate . . .

BLANCHE *(Stops again)* Can't he do that someplace else?

KATE I'll break his arm, that's where he'll do it. *(She calls out)* Eugene, I'm not going to tell you again. Do you hear me?

EUGENE It's the last batter, Mom. Mel Ott is up. It's a crucial moment in World Series history.

KATE Your Aunt Blanche has a splitting headache.

BLANCHE I don't want him to stop playing. It's just the banging.

LAURIE *(Looks up from her book)* He always does it when I'm studying. I have a big test in history tomorrow.

EUGENE   One pitch, Mom? I think I can get him to pop up. I have my stuff today.

KATE   Your father will give you plenty of stuff when he comes home! You hear?

EUGENE   All right! All right!

KATE   I want you inside *now*! Put out the water glasses.

BLANCHE   I can do that.

KATE   Why? Is his arm broken? *(She yells out again)* And I don't want any back talk, you hear?
   (She goes back to the kitchen)

EUGENE   *(Slams the ball into his glove angrily. Then he cups his hand, making a megaphone out of it and announces to the grandstands)*   "Attention, ladeees and gentlemen! Today's game will be delayed because of my Aunt Blanche's headache . . ."

KATE   Blanche, that's enough sewing today. That's all I need is for you to go blind.

BLANCHE   I just have this one edge to finish . . . Laurie, darling, help your Aunt Kate with the dishes.

LAURIE   Two more pages, all right, Ma? I have to finish the Macedonian Wars.

KATE   Always studying, that one. She's gonna have some head on her shoulders. *(She calls out from the kitchen)* Eugene!!

EUGENE   I'm coming.

KATE   And wash your hands.

EUGENE   They're clean. I'm wearing a glove. (*He throws the ball into his glove again . . . then he looks out front and addresses the audience*) I hate my name! Eugene Morris Jerome . . . It is the second worst name ever given to a male child. The first worst is Haskell Fleischmann . . . How am I ever going to play for the Yankees with a name like Eugene Morris Jerome? You have to be a Joe . . . or a Tony . . . or Frankie . . . If only I was born Italian . . . All the best Yankees are Italian . . . My mother makes spaghetti with ketchup, what chance do I have?
      (*He slams the ball into his glove again*)

LAURIE   I'm almost through, Ma.

BLANCHE   All right, darling. Don't get up too quickly.

KATE (*To* LAURIE)   You have better color today, sweetheart. Did you get a little sun this morning?

LAURIE   I walked down to the beach.

BLANCHE   Very slowly, I hope?

LAURIE   Yes, Ma.

BLANCHE   That's good.

EUGENE (*Turns to the audience again*)   She gets all this special treatment because the doctors say she has kind of a flutter in her heart . . . I got hit with a baseball right in the back of the skull, I saw two of everything for a week and I still had to carry a block of ice home every afternoon . . . Girls are treated like queens. Maybe that's what I should have been born—an Italian girl . . .

6

KATE (*Picks up a sweat sock from the floor*)   EUGENE!!

EUGENE   *What??*

KATE   How many times have I told you not to leave your things around the house?

EUGENE   A hundred and nine.

KATE   What?

EUGENE   You said yesterday, "I told you a hundred and nine times not to leave your things around the house."

BLANCHE   Don't be fresh to your mother, Gene!

EUGENE (*To the audience*)   Was I fresh? I swear to God, that's what she said to me yesterday . . . One day I'm going to put all this in a book or a play. I'm going to be a writer like Ring Lardner or somebody—that's if things don't work out first with the Yankees, or the Cubs, or the Red Sox, or maybe possibly the Tigers . . . If I get down to the St. Louis Browns, then I'll definitely be a writer.

LAURIE   Mom, can I have a glass of lemonade?

BLANCHE   It'll spoil your dinner, darling.

KATE   A small glass, it couldn't hurt her.

BLANCHE   All right. In a minute, angel.

KATE   I'll get it. I'm in the kitchen anyway.

EUGENE (*To the audience*)   Can you believe that? She'd better have a bad heart or I'm going to kill her one day . . . (*He gets up to walk into the house, then stops on the porch steps and turns to the audience again . . . confi-*

dentially) Listen, I hope you don't repeat this to anybody . . . What I'm telling you are my secret memoirs. It's called, "The Unbelievable, Fantastic and Completely Private Thoughts of I, Eugene Morris Jerome, in this, the fifteenth year of his life, in the year nineteen hundred and thirty-seven, in the community of Brighton Beach, Borough of Brooklyn, Kings County, City of New York, Empire State of the American Nation—"

KATE *(Comes out of the kitchen with a glass of lemonade and one roller skate)* A roller skate? On my kitchen floor? Do you want me dead, is that what you want?

EUGENE *(Rushes into the house)* I didn't leave it there.

KATE No? Then who? Laurie? Aunt Blanche? Did you ever see them on skates? *(She holds out the skate)* Take this upstairs . . . Come here!

EUGENE *(Approaches, holding the back of his head)* Don't hit my skull, I have a concussion.

KATE *(Handing the glass to* LAURIE*)* What would you tell your father if he came home and I was dead on the kitchen floor?

EUGENE I'd say, "Don't go in the kitchen, Pa!"

KATE *(Swings at him, he ducks and she misses)* Get upstairs! And don't come down with dirty hands.

EUGENE *(Goes up the stairs. He turns to the audience)* You see why I want to write all this down? In case I grow up all twisted and warped, the world will know why.

BLANCHE *(Still sewing)*   He's a boy. He's young. You should be glad he's healthy and active. Before the doctors found out what Laurie had, she was the same way.

KATE   Never. Girls are different. When you and I were girls, we kept the house spotless. It was Ben and Ezra who drove Momma crazy. *(We see* EUGENE, *upstairs, enter his room and take out a notebook and pencil and lie down on his bed, making a new entry in his "memoirs")* . . . I've always been like that. I have to have things clean. Just like Momma. The day they packed up and left the house in Russia, she cleaned the place from top to bottom. She said, "No matter what the Cossacks did to us, when they broke into our house, they would have respect for the Jews."

LAURIE   Who were the Cossacks?

KATE   The same filthy bunch as live across the street.

LAURIE   Across the street? You mean the Murphys?

KATE   *All* of them.

LAURIE   The Murphys are Russian?

BLANCHE   The mother is nice. She's been very sweet to me.

KATE   Her windows are so filthy, I thought she had black curtains hanging inside.

BLANCHE   I was in their house. It was very neat. *Nobody* could be as clean as you.

KATE   What business did you have in their house?

BLANCHE   She invited me for tea.

9

KATE To meet that drunken son of hers?

BLANCHE No. Just the two of us.

KATE I'm living here seven years, she never invited *me* for tea. Because she knows your situation. I know their kind. Remember what Momma used to tell us. "Stay on your own side of the street. That's what they have gutters for."

(*She goes back into the kitchen*)

EUGENE (*Writing, says aloud*) "That's-what-they-have-gutters-for" . . . (*To the audience*) If my mother knew I was writing all this down, she would stuff me like one of her chickens . . . I'd better explain what she meant by Aunt Blanche's "situation." You see, her husband, Uncle Dave, died six years ago from (*He looks around*) this thing . . . They never say the word. They always whisper it. It was (*He whispers*)—cancer! I think they're afraid if they said it out loud, God would say, "I HEARD THAT! YOU SAID THE DREAD DIS-EASE! (*He points his finger down*) JUST FOR THAT, I SMITE YOU DOWN WITH IT!!" . . . There are some things that grownups just won't discuss. For ex-ample, my grandfather. He died from (*He whispers*)—diphtheria! Anyway, after Uncle Dave died, he left Aunt Blanche with no money. Not even insurance. And she couldn't support herself because she has (*He whispers*)—asthma . . . So my big-hearted mother in-sisted we take her and her kids in to live with us. So they broke up our room into two small rooms, and me and my brother Stan live on this side, and Laurie and her sister Nora live on the other side. My father thought it would just be temporary, but it's been three

and a half years so far and I think because of Aunt Blanche's situation, my father is developing *(He whispers)*—high blood pressure!
(He resumes his writing)

KATE *(Comes out of the kitchen with a pitcher and says to* LAURIE*)* Have some more lemonade, dear.

LAURIE *(Sits up)* Thank you, Aunt Kate.

BLANCHE Drink it slowly.

LAURIE I am.

KATE *(Looks at* BLANCHE*)* Blanche, that's enough already. Since seven o'clock this morning.

BLANCHE I was just stopping.

KATE You'll sew your fingers together.

BLANCHE It's getting dark anyway. *(She stops, sits back and rubs her eyes)* I think I need new glasses.

LAURIE Our teacher said you should change them every two years.

KATE *(To* BLANCHE*)* Would it kill you to put a light on?

BLANCHE I don't have to run up electric bills. I owe you and Jack enough as it is.

KATE Have I asked you for anything? You see anybody starving around here? If I go hungry, you'll give me something from your plate.

BLANCHE Kate! I'm going to pay you and Jack back someday. I don't know when, but I keep my word.

KATE   From your lips to the Irish Sweepstakes . . . Go in and taste the soup. See if it needs salt.
   (BLANCHE *goes into the kitchen*)

LAURIE   Should I put out the water glasses or is Eugene going to do it?
   (EUGENE, *having heard, slams his "memoirs" shut angrily*)

KATE (*Yells up*)   EUGENE! It's the last time I'm going to tell you! (*To* LAURIE) Just do the napkins, darling.
   (*She goes into the kitchen.* LAURIE *gets up and starts to set out the napkins*)

EUGENE (*Sits up on his bed and addresses the audience*) Because of her "condition," I have to do twice as much work around here. Boy, if I could just make the Yankees, I'd be in St. Petersburg this winter . . . (*He starts out and down the stairs*) Her sister Nora isn't too bad. She's sixteen. I don't mind her much. (*He is downstairs by now*) At least she's not too bad to look at. (*He starts taking down some glasses from the open cupboard*) To be absolutely honest, this is the year I started noticing girls that weren't too bad to look at. Nora started developing about eight months ago . . . I have the exact date written in my diary.
   (*Suddenly we hear a voice. It is* NORA)

NORA   Mom! Laurie! Aunt Kate! (*We see* NORA, *an absolutely lovely sixteen-and-a-half-year-old girl, with a developed chest, bound across the front steps and into the house. She is bubbling over with enthusiasm*) I've got incredible news, everybody!!

EUGENE Hi, Nora!

NORA Eugene! My sweet adorable handsome cousin! Wait'll I tell you what's happened to me. *(She throws her arms around him, hugs him close and kisses his cheek. Then she rushes into the other room to* LAURIE*)* I'm fainting! I'm absolutely fainting!

EUGENE *(Still stunned from the hug, turns to the audience)* I felt her chest! When she grabbed me, I felt my first chest.

NORA I can't believe this whole day!

LAURIE What happened?

NORA Where's Mom? Aunt Kate? I have to tell everyone. *(She rushes to the kitchen door)* Everybody inside for the big news!
     *(*KATE *and* BLANCHE *come out of the kitchen.* KATE *is mashing potatoes in a pot)*

KATE What's all the excitement?

BLANCHE You're all red in the face.

NORA Sit down, Mom, because I don't want you fainting on the floor.

KATE Sit down, Blanche.

LAURIE Mom, sit down.
     *(*BLANCHE *sits)*

NORA You too, Aunt Kate. Okay. Is everybody ready?

LAURIE Stop dragging it out. The suspense is *killing* me.

BLANCHE   Don't say things like that, Laurie.

KATE *(To the others)*   Can I hear what the girl has to say? *(To* NORA*)* Go ahead, darling.

NORA *(A little breathless)*   Okay! Here goes! . . . I'm going to be in a Broadway show! *(They look at her in a stunned silence)* It's a musical called *Abracadabra*. This man, Mr. Beckman, he's a producer, came to our dancing class this afternoon and he picked out three girls. We have to be at the Hudson Theater on Monday morning at ten o'clock to audition for the dance director. But on the way out he took me aside and said the job was as good as mine. I have to call him tomorrow. I may have to go into town to talk to him about it. They start rehearsing a week from Monday and then it goes to Philadelphia, Wilmington and Washington . . . and then it comes to New York the second week in December. There are nine big musical numbers and there's going to be a big tank on the stage that you can see through and the big finale all takes place with the entire cast all under water . . . I mean, can you believe it? I'm going to be in a Broadway show, Momma!
   (They are all still stunned)

BLANCHE *(To* KATE*)*   What is she talking about?

KATE   Do I know? Am I her mother?

LAURIE   How can you be in a show? Don't you have to sing and act?

NORA   I can sing.

LAURIE   No, you can't.

NORA A little.

LAURIE No, you can't.

NORA I can carry a *tune.*

LAURIE No, you can't.

NORA Well, I probably won't have to. They're just looking for dancers.

LAURIE On Broadway you have to sing and act.

NORA How do *you* know? You never saw a Broadway show.

BLANCHE Did you tell him how old you were?

NORA He didn't ask me.

BLANCHE He didn't ask if you were sixteen?

NORA He just asked me to audition. My God, isn't anybody excited?

EUGENE I am. It's the most fantastic thing I ever heard.

NORA Thanks, Eugene. I'm glad somebody's excited.

EUGENE (*Turns to the audience*) My God! I'll be sleeping right next door to a *show girl*!

BLANCHE How can you go to Philadelphia? What about school?

NORA School? Momma, this is a Broadway show. This is what I want to do with my life. Algebra and English isn't going to help me on the stage.

LAURIE *Aren't?*

NORA   Will you stay out of this!

BLANCHE   You mean not finish school? Not get a diploma? Do you know how hard it is today for a girl to get a good job without a high school diploma?

NORA   But I've *got* a job. And I'll be making more money than *ten* girls with diplomas.

LAURIE   You don't have it yet. You still have to audition.

NORA   It's as good as mine. Mr. Beckman told me.

BLANCHE   And what if you, God forbid, broke a leg? Or got heavy . . . How long do you think they'll keep you? Dancing is just for a few years. A diploma is forever. I know. I never had one. I know how hard it is to find a decent job. Aunt Kate knows. Tell her, Kate.

KATE   It's very hard.

NORA   Then why did you send me to dancing school for three years? Why do I spend two hours a day on a subway, four days a week after school, with money that you make going half blind over a broken sewing machine? Why, Momma?

BLANCHE   Because it's my pleasure . . . Because I know how you love it . . . Because you asked me.

NORA   Then I'm asking you something else, Momma. Let me do something for *you* now. I could be making almost sixty dollars a week. Maybe even more . . . In two years when I get out of high school, I wouldn't make that much with a *college* diploma.

BLANCHE (*Takes a deep breath*) I can't think now. It's almost dinnertime. Uncle Jack will be home soon. We'll discuss it later.
(*She gets up*)

NORA I have to know *now*, Momma. I have to call Mr. Beckman and let him know if I can go to the audition on Monday . . . At least let me audition. Let me find out first if they think I'm good enough. Please don't say no until Monday.
(*They all look at* BLANCHE. *She looks down at her hands*)

EUGENE (*Turns toward the audience*) It was a tense moment for everybody . . . I love tense moments! Especially when I'm not the one they're all tense about.
(*He turns back and looks at* BLANCHE)

BLANCHE Well, God knows we can use the money. We all owe Aunt Kate and Uncle Jack enough as it is . . . I think they have as much say in this as I do. How do you feel about it, Kate?

KATE (*Shrugs*) Me? I never voted before in my life, why should I start with my own family? . . . I have to heat up the potatoes.
(*She goes into the kitchen*)

BLANCHE Then we'll leave it up to Uncle Jack. We'll let him make the decision.
(*She starts for the kitchen*)

NORA Why, Momma? I love him but he's not my father.

BLANCHE   Because I need help. Because I don't always know what the right thing to do is . . . Because I say so, that's why.

(*She goes into the kitchen, leaving* LAURIE *and* EUGENE *standing there staring at the forlorn* NORA)

EUGENE   Eugene M. Jerome of New York casts one vote for "yes." (NORA *looks up at him, breaks into tears and runs out of the room and up the stairs.* LAURIE *follows her up. He turns toward the audience*) What I'm about to tell you next is so secret and private that I've left instructions for my memoirs not to be opened until thirty years after my death . . . I, Eugene M. Jerome, have committed a mortal sin by lusting after my cousin Nora. I can tell you all this now because I'll be dead when you're reading it . . . If I had my choice between a tryout with the Yankees and actually seeing her bare breasts for two and a half seconds, I would have some serious thinking to do . . .

KATE   (*Comes out of the kitchen*)   I need bread.

EUGENE   (*Turns quickly*)   What?

KATE   I don't have enough bread. Run across the street to Greenblatt's and get a fresh rye bread.

EUGENE   Again? I went to the store this morning.

KATE   So you'll go again this afternoon.

EUGENE   I'm always going to the store. When I grow up, that's all I'll be trained to do, go to the store.

KATE   You don't want to go? . . . Never mind, I'll go.

EUGENE *Don't* do that! Don't make me feel guilty. I'll go.

KATE And get a quarter pound of butter.

EUGENE I bought a quarter pound of butter this morning. Why don't you buy a half pound at a time?

KATE And suppose the house burned down this afternoon? Why do I need an extra quarter pound of butter? *(She goes back into the kitchen)*

EUGENE *(Turns toward the audience)* If my mother taught logic in high school, this would be some weird country.
(He runs out of the house to Greenblatt's. Our attention goes to the two girls upstairs in their room. NORA is crying. LAURIE sits on the twin bed opposite her, watching)

LAURIE So? What are you going to do?

NORA I don't know. Leave me alone. Don't just sit there watching me.

LAURIE It's my room as much as yours. I don't have to leave if I don't want to.

NORA Do you have to stare at me? Can't I have any privacy?

LAURIE I'm staring into space. I can't help it if your body interferes. *(There is a pause)* I bet you're worried?

NORA How would you feel if your entire life depended on what your Uncle Jack decided? . . . Oh, God, I wish Daddy were alive.

LAURIE   He would have said "No." He was really *strict*.

NORA   Not with me. I mean, he was strict but he was fair. If he said "No," he always gave you a good reason. He always talked things out . . . I wish I could call him somewhere now and ask him what to do. One three-minute call to heaven is all I ask.

LAURIE   Ask Mom. She talks to him every night.

NORA   Who told you that?

LAURIE   She did. Every night before she goes to bed. She puts his picture on her pillow and talks to him. Then she pulls the blanket halfway up the picture and goes to sleep.

NORA   She does not.

LAURIE   She does too. Last year when I had the big fever, I slept in bed with the both of them. In the middle of the night, my face fell on his picture and cut my nose.

NORA   She never told me that . . . That's weird.

LAURIE   I can't remember him much anymore. I used to remember him real good but now he disappears a little bit every day.

NORA   Oh, God, he was so handsome. Always dressed so dapper, his shoes always shined. I always thought he should have been a movie star . . . like Gary Cooper . . . only very short. Mostly I remember his pockets.

LAURIE   His pockets?

NORA   When I was six or seven he always brought me home a little surprise. Like a Hershey or a top. He'd tell me to go get it in his coat pocket. So I'd run to the closet and put my hand in and it felt as big as a tent. I wanted to crawl in there and go to sleep. And there were all these terrific things in there, like Juicy Fruit gum or Spearmint Life Savers and bits of cellophane and crumbled pieces of tobacco and movie stubs and nickels and pennies and rubber bands and paper clips and his gray suede gloves that he wore in the wintertime.

LAURIE   With the stitched lines down the fingers. I remember.

NORA   Then I found his coat in Mom's closet and I put my hand in the pocket. And everything was gone. It was emptied and dry-cleaned and it felt cold . . . And that's when I knew he was really dead. (*She thinks for a moment*) Oh, God, I wish we had our own place to live. I hate being a boarder. Listen, let's make a pact . . . The first one who makes enough money promises not to spend any on herself, but saves it all to get a house for you and me and Mom. That means every penny we get from now on, we save for the house. We can't buy *anything*. No lipstick or magazines or nail polish or bubble gum. *Nothing* . . . Is it a pact?

LAURIE   (*Thinks*)   What about movies?

NORA   Movies too.

LAURIE   Starting when?

NORA   Starting today. Starting right now.

LAURIE   Can we start Sunday? I wanted to see *The Thin Man.*

NORA   Who's in it?

LAURIE   William Powell and Myrna Loy.

NORA   Okay. Starting Sunday . . . I'll go with you Saturday.

(They shake hands, sealing their "pact," then both lie down in their respective beds and stare up at the ceiling, contemplating their "future home.")

EUGENE *returns with a paper bag containing the milk and butter under his arm. He stops, pretends to be a quarterback awaiting the pass from center. The bread is his football)*

EUGENE   Sid Luckman of Columbia waits for the snap from center, the snow is coming down in a near blizzard, he gets it, he fades back, he passes *(He acts all this out)*—AND LUCKMAN'S GOT IT! LUCKMAN CATCHES HIS OWN PASS! HE'S ON THE FIFTY, THE FORTY, THE THIRTY, THE TWENTY . . . IT'S A TOUCHDOWN! Columbia wins! They defeat the mighty Crimson of Harvard, thirteen to twelve. Listen to that crowd!

(He roars like a crowd . . .)

KATE *(Comes out of the kitchen. She yells out)*   EUGENE! STOP THAT YELLING! I HAVE A CAKE IN THE OVEN!

(She goes back into the kitchen. STANLEY JEROME appears. STAN is eighteen and a half. He wears slacks, a shirt and tie, a zip-up jacket and a cap)

STAN *(In half whisper)*   Hey! Eugie!

EUGENE Hi, Stan! *(To the audience)* My brother Stan. He's okay. You'll like him. *(To STAN)* What are you doing home so early?

STAN *(Looks around, lowers his voice)* Is Pop home yet?

EUGENE No . . . Did you ask about the tickets?

STAN What tickets?

EUGENE For the Yankee game. You said your boss knew this guy who could get passes. You didn't ask him?

STAN Me and my boss had other things to talk about. *(He sits on the steps, his head down, almost in tears)* I'm in trouble, Eug. I mean, really big trouble.

EUGENE *(To the audience)* This really shocked me. Because Stan is the kind of guy who could talk himself out of *any* kind of trouble. *(To STAN)* What kind of trouble?

STAN I got fired today!

EUGENE *(Shocked)* Fired? You mean for good?

STAN You don't get fired temporarily. It's permanent. It's a lifetime firing.

EUGENE Why? What happened?

STAN It was on account of Andrew. The colored guy who sweeps up. Well, he was cleaning the floor in the stockroom and he lays his broom against the table to put some junk in the trash can and the broom slips, knocks a can of linseed oil over the table and ruins three brand-new hats right out of the box. Nine-dollar Stetsons. It wasn't his fault. He didn't put the linseed oil there, right?

EUGENE   Right.

STAN   So Mr. Stroheim sees the oily hats and he gets crazy. He says to Andrew the hats are going to have to come out of his salary. Twenty-seven dollars. So Andrew starts to cry.

EUGENE   He cried?

STAN   Forty-two years old, he's bawling all over the stockroom. I mean, the man hasn't got too much furniture upstairs anyway, but he's real sweet. He brings me coffee, always laughing, telling me jokes. I never understand them but I laugh anyway, make him feel good, you know?

EUGENE   Yeah?

STAN   Anyway, I said to Mr. Stroheim I didn't think that was fair. It wasn't Andrew's fault.

EUGENE   (*Astounded*)   You said that to him?

STAN   Sure, why not? So Mr. Stroheim says, "You wanna pay for the hats, big mouth?" So I said, "No. I don't want to pay for the hats." So he says, "Then mind your own business, big mouth."

EUGENE   Holy mackerel.

STAN   So Mr. Stroheim looks at me like machine-gun bullets are coming out of his eyes. And then he calmly sends Andrew over to the factory to pick up three new hats. Which is usually my job. So guess what Mr. Stroheim tells *me* to do?

EUGENE   What?

STAN   He tells me to sweep up. He says, for this week I'm the cleaning man.

EUGENE   I can't believe it.

STAN   Everybody is watching me now, waiting to see what I'm going to do. (EUGENE *nods in agreement*) Even Andrew stopped crying and watched. I felt the dignity of everyone who worked in that store was in my hands. So I grit my teeth and I pick up the broom, and there's this big pile of dirt right in the middle of the floor . . .

EUGENE   Yeah?

STAN   . . . and I sweep it all over Mr. Stroheim's shoes. Andrew had just finished shining them this morning, if you want to talk about irony.

EUGENE   I'm dying. I'm actually dying.

STAN (*Enjoying himself*)   You could see everyone in the place is about to bust a gut. Mrs. Mulcahy, the bookkeeper, can hardly keep her false teeth in her mouth. Andrew's eyes are hanging five inches out of their sockets.

EUGENE   This is the greatest story in the history of the world.

STAN   So Mr. Stroheim grabs me and pulls me into his back office, closes the door and pulls down the shades. He gives me this whole story how he was brought up in Germany to respect his superiors. That if he ever— (*With an accent*) "did soch a ting like you do, dey would beat me in der kopf until dey carried me avay dead."

EUGENE   That's perfect. You got him down perfect.

STAN   And I say, "Yeah. But we're not in Germany, old buddy."

EUGENE   You said that to him?

STAN   No. To myself. I didn't want to go too far.

EUGENE   I was wondering.

STAN   Anyway, he says he's always liked me and always thought I was a good boy and that he was going to give me one more chance. He wants a letter of apology. And that if the letter of apology isn't on his desk by nine o'clock tomorrow morning, I can consider myself fired.

EUGENE   I would have had a heart attack . . . What did you say?

STAN   I said I was not going to apologize if Andrew still had to pay for the hats . . . He said that was between him and Andrew, and that he expected the letter from me in the morning . . . I said good night, walked out of his office, got my hat and went home . . . ten minutes early.

EUGENE   I'm sweating. I swear to God, I'm sweating all over.

STAN   I don't know why I did it. But I got so mad. It just wasn't fair. I mean, if you give in when you're eighteen and a half, you'll give in for the rest of your life, don't you think?

EUGENE   I suppose so . . . So what's the decision? Are you going to write the letter?

STAN   *(Thinks)*   . . . No!

EUGENE   Positively?

STAN   Positively. Except I'll have to discuss it with Pop. I know we need the money. But he told me once, you always have to do what you think is right in this world and stand up for your principles.

EUGENE   And what if he says he thinks you're wrong? That you should write the letter.

STAN   He won't. He's gonna leave it up to me, I know it.

EUGENE   But what if he says, "Write the letter"?

STAN   Well, that's something we won't know until after dinner, will we?
    (He walks into the house)

EUGENE   *(Looks after him, then turns to the audience)*   All in all, it was shaping up to be one heck of a dinner. I'll say this though—I always had this two-way thing about my brother. Either I worshiped the ground he

walked on or I hated him so much I wanted to kill him
. . . I guess you know how I feel about him today.
(He walks into the house as KATE *comes out of the
kitchen carrying a water pitcher for the table.* STAN
has stopped to look at the small pile of mail)

KATE *(To* EUGENE*)*   All day it takes to bring home bread?
Give Aunt Blanche the butter, she's waiting for it.

EUGENE   I was home a half-hour ago. I was talking to
Stan.

(He goes into the kitchen)

STAN   Hey, I got a letter from Rosalyn Weiner. Remember her? She moved to Manhattan. They live up on
Central Park West.

KATE   Why not? Her father's a gangster, her mother is
worse. I don't get a kiss "Hello"?

STAN   Nope. I was going to save it up and give you a
giant one for Christmas.

KATE   We don't have Christmas. I'll take it now, thank
you. *(He puts his arms around her and kisses her warmly,
then embraces her)* A hug too? When do I ever get a hug
from you? You must have done something wrong.

STAN   You're too smart for me, Mom. I robbed a barbershop today.

KATE   Is that why you look so tired? You don't get
enough sleep. Running around all night with your two
hundred girl friends.

STAN   A hundred and thirty. That's all I have, a hundred
and thirty.

KATE How do you get any work done?

STAN I get it done.

KATE And your boss doesn't say anything to you? About being tired?

STAN About being tired? No. He doesn't.
(*He starts toward the stairs*)

KATE Did you ask him about Thursday?

STAN What?

KATE You were going to ask him about getting paid this Thursday so I can pay Greenblatt's on Friday. Saturday is a holiday.

STAN Oh. No. I forgot . . . I'll ask him tomorrow.

KATE If it's a problem, don't ask him. Greenblatt can wait. Your boss is more important.

STAN That's not true, Mom. My boss isn't any more important than Mr. Greenblatt.
(*He goes upstairs and on to his room, where he lies down, tries to read his letter, then puts it down and stares up at the ceiling wondering about his predicament.*
EUGENE *bursts out of the kitchen and practically staggers out of the house. He sits on the steps, his head down, looking very disconsolate. He addresses the audience*)

EUGENE Oh, God! As if things weren't bad enough . . . and now this! The ultimate tragedy . . . liver and cabbage for dinner! A Jewish medieval torture! . . . My friend Marty Gregorio, an A student in science, told me that cooked cabbage can be smelled farther than sound traveling for seven minutes. If these memoirs are never finished, you'll know it's because I gagged to death one night in the middle of supper. (*We suddenly hear a crash of broken dishes in the kitchen.* EUGENE *turns toward the sound, then to the audience*) You're all witnesses. I was sitting here, right? But I'll get blamed for that, anyway.

(*The kitchen door opens and* KATE *comes out helping* BLANCHE, *who is wheezing and gasping quite badly. She can't catch her breath*)

BLANCHE   I'm all right. Just let me sit a minute.

KATE   Didn't I tell you to get out of that hot kitchen? *I* can't breathe in there and *I* don't have asthma. (*She calls out*) NORA! LAURIE! Come help your mother!!
(NORA *and* LAURIE *jump up from their beds*)

BLANCHE   I'm sick about the plates. I'll replace them. Don't worry about the plates.

KATE   Plates I can always get. I only have one sister.
(*The girls have come down the stairs*)

NORA   What happened?

BLANCHE   I'm all right. Don't run, Laurie.

KATE   It's another asthma attack. It's the second one this week. Nora, maybe you'd better get the doctor.

BLANCHE   I don't need doctors . . .

KATE   This is no climate for you, near the beach. What you need is someplace dry.

LAURIE   Like Arizona, Momma.

NORA   Should I get the doctor?

BLANCHE   No. No doctors. It's better. It's going away.

LAURIE   I can still hear the whistle.

NORA   Will you shut up!

BLANCHE   (*To* NORA)   Help Aunt Kate in the kitchen, Nora. I broke her good plates.

KATE   Never mind—Eugene will do it. You go up and get your mother's medicine . . . Laurie, you sit there quiet and watch your mother. You look pale as a ghost. Eugene!

EUGENE and KATE   Come in here and help me!

JACK   (*Offstage*)   Hello, Mrs. Kresky, how are you?

EUGENE   (*Gets up, looks off down the street*)   In a minute, Ma. Pop's home!

LAURIE   (*Sits next to her mother. To the audience*)   I would now like to introduce my father, a real hard worker. He was born at the age of forty-two . . . Hi, Pop! How you doin', Pop?

> (JACOB "JACK" JEROME *appears, a man about forty, who could pass for older. He wears a wrinkled suit, brown felt hat and black shoes. The* Brooklyn Eagle *sticks up out of his side coat pocket. He carries two large and very heavy cardboard boxes, tied around with hemp cord. He appears to be very tired*)

JACK   How am I doin'?

EUGENE   Let me carry these for you, Pop.
   (He reaches for one of the boxes)

JACK   They're too heavy, you'll hurt yourself.

EUGENE   No. I can do it easy. *(He takes one of the boxes, tries to lift it. It weighs a ton)* Ugh! I just have to get a good grip.
   (JACK stops and sits. He wipes his forehead with a handkerchief and holds his chest)

JACK   I want to sit a few minutes.

EUGENE   Are you okay, Pop?

JACK   I'm resting, that's all . . . Get me a glass of cold water.

EUGENE   *(Struggles with the first box toward the house)*   I'll be out for the other box in a minute, Pop. *(To the audience)* I don't know how he does it. King Kong couldn't lift these . . . You know what's in here? Noise-makers and party favors. Pop sells them to night clubs and hotels after he gets through every day with his regular work, which is cutting material for ladies' rain-coats.

JACK   Did you do your homework today?

EUGENE   Not all of it. Mom sent me to the store fifteen times. *Amos 'n' Andy* is on tonight.

JACK   Do your homework, then we'll discuss *Amos 'n' Andy.*
   (EUGENE continues into the house as NORA comes down the stairs with her mother's medicine)

NORA   Here's your medicine, Mom. Laurie, go get some water.

BLANCHE   Laurie shouldn't be running.

EUGENE (*The hero*)   I'll get it, Nora.

NORA   You sure you don't mind?

EUGENE   No. No trouble at all. (*To the audience*) Two and a half seconds, that's all I ask. (*He goes into the kitchen*)

NORA (*To* BLANCHE)   When are you going to speak to Uncle Jack, Mom?

BLANCHE   When I speak to him, that's when I'll speak to him.

NORA   Tonight? I have to know tonight.

BLANCHE   I'll see . . . If he's not too tired, I'll talk to him tonight.

KATE (*Comes out of the kitchen*)   Jack's home. We'll eat in ten minutes. Nora, darling, go get Stanley . . . How's your mother, Laurie?

LAURIE   Much better. The whistling's stopped.
   (KATE *walks to the front door and goes out.* JACK *is sitting on the stoop, wiping his neck.* NORA *goes upstairs*)

KATE   What's wrong? Eugene said you were holding your chest.

JACK   I wasn't holding my chest.

KATE   You have to carry that box every day? Back and forth to the city. You don't work hard enough, Jack?

JACK   You want the box, it's yours. Keep it. I don't need it anymore.

KATE   What do you mean?

JACK   Del Mars Party Favors went out of business. They closed him out. The man is bankrupt.

KATE   Oh, my God!

JACK   He never even warned me it was coming.

KATE   You told me he lived up on Riverside Drive. With a view of the river. A three-hundred-dollar-a-month apartment he had. A man like that.

JACK   Who are the ones you think go bankrupt? You live in a cold-water flat on Delancey Street, bankruptcy is the one thing God spares you.

KATE   All right . . . You can always find good in something. You don't have to lug that box anymore. You don't have to get up at five-thirty in the morning. We can all eat dinner at a decent hour. You still have your job with Jacobson, we won't starve.

JACK   I can't make ends meet with what I make at Jacobson's. Not with seven people to feed.

KATE   (*Looks back toward the house*)   They'll hear you. We'll talk later.

JACK   I can't get by without that extra twenty-five dollars a week. I can't pay rent and insurance and food and clothing for seven people. Christmas and New Year's alone I made a hundred and fifty dollars.

KATE (*Nervous about someone hearing*) Stop it, Jack. You'll only get yourself sick.

JACK He didn't even pay me for the week, the bastard. Five salesmen are laid off and he's going to a Broadway show tonight. I stuffed every hat and noisemaker I could carry in that box and walked out of there. At his funeral I'll put on a pointy hat and blow a horn, the bastard!

KATE Don't talk like that. Something'll come up. You'll go to temple this weekend. You'll pray all day Saturday.

JACK (*Smiles ironically*) There's men in that temple who've been praying for forty years. You know how many prayers have to get answered before my turn comes up?

KATE (*Rubs his back where it pains him*) Your turn'll come up. God has time for everybody.
(EUGENE *has come out of the kitchen with two glasses of water. He walks over to* BLANCHE)

EUGENE Here's your water, Aunt Blanche.

BLANCHE Thank you, darling.

EUGENE Where's Nora?

LAURIE She went up to call Stanley for dinner.

EUGENE Hey, Laurie—you want to take a walk on the beach tonight?

35

LAURIE I have homework. What do you want to walk with me for?

EUGENE You, me and Nora. I just felt like taking a walk.

LAURIE I think Nora has a date with Larry Clurman.

EUGENE *Larry Clurman??* She likes Larry Clurman?

LAURIE I don't know. Ask her yourself.

EUGENE Larry Clurman is my father's age.

LAURIE He's twenty.

EUGENE Same thing . . . You think he's good-looking?

LAURIE I don't think *anybody's* good-looking.

EUGENE Larry Clurman? He doesn't even have a chin. His tie comes all the way up to his teeth.

KATE *(Calls out)* Eugene! Where's your father's water?

EUGENE I'm coming! I'm coming. *(As he walks through the front door, he turns to the audience)* Now I've got Larry Clurman to contend with. *(He comes out)* Here's your water, Pop. I put ice in it.
  (He hands a glass of water to his father, who drinks it all)

KATE Don't drink so fast.

EUGENE Do you have time to look at my sneakers, Pop?

KATE What does he want to look at your sneakers for?

EUGENE   They have no soles. They're hanging on by a tiny piece of rubber. I have to clench my toes when I run out for a fly ball.

JACK   I bought you new sneakers last month.

EUGENE   Last year, Pa. Not last month. I can only wear them two hours a day because my toes can't grow in them.

KATE   This is no time to talk to your father about sneakers. He's got enough on his mind. Turn the light down on the liver. (EUGENE *goes inside and into the kitchen. To* JACK) We'll talk about this tonight. You'll eat a nice dinner, relax, and when everybody's asleep, we'll figure things out calmly. I don't like it when you get upset.

BLANCHE   I'm feeling better. Come, dear, help me with dinner.

JACK (*Looks at the house*)   You think she'll ever get married?

KATE   Blanche?

JACK   She's not unattractive. I see men look at her on the beach. What does she want to waste her life in this house for?

KATE   She's raising two children.

JACK   Why doesn't she ever go out? If she wants to meet people, I know plenty of single men.

KATE   Blanche isn't the type to get married.

JACK She was married once, wasn't she? Those are the type that get married.

KATE Dave was different. She's not interested in other men.

JACK What about that Murphy fellow across the street? He's plenty interested, believe me.

KATE That drunk! The man can't find his way into the house at night. He slept in the doorway once. In the rain. He was there when I went out to get the milk.

JACK He's got a good-paying job, lives alone with his mother. So he takes a drink on a Saturday night. Maybe what he needs is a good woman.

KATE Not my sister. Let him meet someone lying in the next doorway. I don't want to discuss this anymore. *(She goes inside and into the kitchen. JACK sighs, gets up slowly and follows her in. Our attention goes to STANLEY on his bed still reading the letter from Rosalyn Weiner. He suddenly sits up. NORA knocks on the door)*

STANLEY Come in.

NORA *(Entering)* Are you busy? I wanted to talk to you.

STANLEY That's funny, because I wanted to talk to *you.*

NORA About what?

STANLEY I need a favor. Real bad. You're the only one who can help me.

NORA What is it?

STANLEY   Well, when Pop comes home tired, he doesn't usually pay too much attention to me and Eugene. He's different with you. He's always interested in what you have to say.

NORA   Really? I hope so.

STANLEY   Oh, sure. You never noticed that?

NORA   Not really. What's the favor?

STANLEY   This may sound dumb, but at dinner, do you think you could steer the conversation in a certain direction?

NORA   What direction?

STANLEY   Well, something like how much you "admire people who stand up for their principles."

NORA   *What* people?

STANLEY   *Any* people. "Principles" is the important word. If you could work it in three or four times, I'd be very grateful.

NORA   Three or four times??

STANLEY   It'll be easy. I'll mention someone like Abraham Lincoln and you look up and say, "Now there's a man who really stood up for his principles."

NORA   I have my *own* things to bring up at dinner. I don't want to get into a discussion about Abraham Lincoln.

STANLEY   Not his whole life. Just his principles.

NORA   Why would I do such a stupid thing?

STANLEY   Because as of tomorrow I'm unemployed
. . . unless someone besides me mentions "sticking up
for your principles."

NORA   What happened? Did you get fired?

STANLEY   I will be unless I write Kaiser Wilhelm a letter
of apology. It's really up to my old man. I've decided
to do whatever he tells me . . .

NORA   When are you going to ask him?

STANLEY   Tonight. Right after dinner.

NORA   *Tonight?* Does it have to be tonight?

STANLEY   That's the deadline. I have to give my answer
to Mr. Stroheim in the morning. Why?

NORA   Couldn't you ask your father in the morning?

STANLEY   He gets up at five-thirty. My mother has to
line up his shoes at night because he can't make decisions at five-thirty. *(She is about to break into tears)*
What's wrong, Nora?

NORA *(Angrily)*   I don't know what *you* have to com-
plain about. At least your father is alive and around
the house to make decisions. You don't know when
you're well off, Stanley. Sometimes you make me
sick!
      *(She runs out of the room, slamming the door behind
      her.* STANLEY *sits there looking bewildered.*

      EUGENE *walks into the dining room facing the audi-
      ence. He looks at them and speaks)*

EUGENE Chapter Seven—"The Infamous Dinner"! (*The others drift into the dining room, taking their seats.* BLANCHE *and* KATE *bring most of the dishes, passing them around. They are all seated as he continues his narrative*) It started out like a murder mystery in Blenheim Castle. No one said a word but everyone looked suspicious . . . It was so quiet, you could hear Laurie's soup going down her esophagus. (*They sit silent, eating*) Everyone had one eye on their plate and the other eye on Pop. Except me. I sat opposite Nora. (*He sits opposite* NORA) I kept dropping my napkin a lot so I could bend down to get a good look at those virginal creamy-white legs. She was really deep in thought because she left herself unguarded a few times and I got to see halfway up her thighs that led to the Golden Palace of the Himalayas.

KATE Eugene! Keep your napkin on your lap and stop daydreaming.

EUGENE (*To the audience*) Stanley knew what I was doing because he's the one who taught it to me. But he was busy with his own problems, like everyone else. You could hear the clock ticking in the kitchen. The tension in the air was so thick, you could cut it with a knife. Which is more than I could say for the liver.
(*He tries to cut his liver*)

JACK Ketchup . . . mustard . . . pickles . . .

EUGENE I'm through. I'll help with the dessert.

KATE Finish your liver.

EUGENE I finished. Do you see liver on my plate?

KATE   You buried it under the mashed potatoes. I know your tricks. Look how Laurie ate hers.

EUGENE *(To the audience)*   I had a major problem. One more bite and I would have thrown up on the table. That's a sight Nora would have remembered forever. A diversion was my only escape from humiliation. *(To* STANLEY*)* So how's things down at Stroheim's, Stanley? *(*STANLEY, *who is drinking water, slams down the glass, splashing it. He glares at* EUGENE, *who continues to address the audience)* I felt bad about that, but for the moment, attention had shifted away from my liver.

JACK *(To* STANLEY*)*   How long have you been working there now?

STANLEY   Where?

JACK   At Stroheim's.

STANLEY   At Stroheim's? Let me see . . . part-time a year and a half before I graduated high school. And a year since then.

JACK   So what's that?

STANLEY   Two and a half years, counting part-time.

JACK   And he likes you?

STANLEY   Who?

JACK *(Impatiently)*   Mr. Stroheim.

STANLEY   Yeah. Usually he likes me. Sometimes I'm not sure.

JACK   You come in on time?

STANLEY   Yeah.

JACK   You do your work?

STANLEY   Yeah.

JACK   You get along with the other people?

STANLEY   Yeah.

JACK   So why shouldn't he like you? How much are you making now?

STANLEY   Seventeen dollars a week.

JACK   It's time you moved up. Tomorrow you go in and ask him for a raise.

STANLEY   A RAISE???

JACK   If you don't speak up, people take advantage of you. Tomorrow morning you go into his office, you're polite, you're respectful, but you're firm. You tell him you think you're worth another five dollars a week.

STANLEY   *FIVE DOLLARS????*

JACK   He'll offer you a dollar and a quarter, you settle for two-fifty. I know how these things work. You're a high school graduate, he's lucky he's got you.

STANLEY   I don't think this is the time to ask him for a raise, Pop. I think his wife is very sick.

JACK   You're afraid to ask him? You want me to take you by the hand and walk into his office and say, "My little boy wants a raise"?

STANLEY   I'm not afraid.

KATE   Your father wouldn't ask you if he didn't think it was the right thing. Believe me, Stanley, now is the time to ask for it.

EUGENE *(Choking)*   Ma, I think I have a bone in my throat.

KATE   There are no bones in liver.
(He runs into the kitchen)

LAURIE   So what's new at dancing school, Nora?

NORA *(Glares at her)*   *Nothing* is new. Mind your own business.

LAURIE   I'm just trying to introduce the subject.

NORA   I don't need your help. Will you tell her to be quiet, Mother.

BLANCHE   Laurie, you may be excused if you're finished.

JACK   What happened at dancing school?

BLANCHE   Nora received a very nice compliment from her teacher. She said Nora had professional potential.

LAURIE   He didn't say "potential." "Potential" is the future. Mr. Beckman is interested in Nora's "immediate present."

JACK *(Still eating)*   Isn't that something! Mr. Beckman is your teacher?

NORA   No. He's one of the most widely known and respected producers on Broadway.

JACK   Broadway? Imagine that. That's wonderful. And how are you doing in school otherwise?

NORA (*Looks at her mother*)   I'm doing fine.

BLANCHE   She's doing very well.

LAURIE   I wish *I* was as smart as she is.

EUGENE   Isn't that the same Mr. Beckman who's producing the great Broadway extravaganza *Abracadabra*? I hear if a girl gets hired for the chorus of a show like that, not only is her career practically guaranteed, but the experience she gains is equal to a four-year college education.

KATE   Eugene, that's enough.

JACK   Only a four-year college education is equal to a four-year college education.

STANLEY   I don't think Abraham Lincoln went to college.
    (NORA *goes into the kitchen*)

JACK   What about you, Laurie? You're feeling all right?

LAURIE   Yes, Uncle Jack.

JACK   You getting plenty of fresh air?
    (NORA *returns*)

LAURIE   As much as I can hold in my lungs. Nora, did you tell Uncle Jack about the big tank that's filled with water?

BLANCHE   Girls, why don't we just let Uncle Jack eat his dinner? If we have something to discuss, we can discuss it later.

JACK   Somebody has something to discuss? If there's a problem, this is the time to bring it up. This is the family hour.

EUGENE   What a great idea for a radio show. *The Family Hour.* Every Wednesday night you hear a different family eating dinner discussing their problems of the week. And you get to hear different recipes. *(As announcer)* "WEAF presents dinner at Brighton Beach starring the Jacob Jerome Family and featuring tonight's specialty, liver and cabbage, brought to you by Ex-Lax, the mild laxative."

KATE   The whole country's going to hear about a fifteen-year-old boy gagging on liver?

JACK   Nothing to discuss? Nobody has any problems? Otherwise I want to turn on the news.

STANLEY   Well, as a matter of fact . . .

JACK   What?

STANLEY   Nothing.

EUGENE   I'll help with the dishes.

KATE   You sit there and finish your liver.

EUGENE   I can't swallow it. It won't go down. Remember the lima-bean catastrophe last month? Does anybody want to see a repeat of that disgusting episode?

JACK   Why does he always talk like it's a Sherlock Holmes story?

STANLEY   He thinks he's a writer.

EUGENE   And what do you think *you* are?

KATE   Eat half of it.

EUGENE   Which half? They're both terrible.

KATE   A quarter of it. Two bites.

EUGENE   *One* bite.

KATE   *Two* bites.

EUGENE   I know you. If I eat one bite, you'll make me eat another bite . . . I'll take it to my room. I'll eat it tonight. I need time to chew it.

JACK   These are not times to waste food. If you didn't want it, Eugene, you shouldn't have taken it.

EUGENE   I didn't take it. They gave it to me. It comes attached to the plate.

NORA   If it's so important to everybody, I'll eat your liver, Eugene.
(*They all look at her*)

EUGENE   You *will*?

NORA   It seems to be the only thing this family is worried about. (*She takes his plate*) Give me your liver so we can get on with more important things in our lives.

JACK   Nora's right. Take the liver away. If nobody likes it, why do you make it?

KATE (*Angrily*)   Because we can't afford a roast beef for seven people.
(*She heads for the kitchen*)

EUGENE *(To the audience)* I suddenly felt vulgar and cheap.

JACK Stanley, turn on the news.

BLANCHE Laurie, get off your feet. You look tired to me.

STANLEY Can I talk to you a minute, Pop? It's something really important.

JACK More important than what's going on in Europe? *(He turns on the radio)*

STANLEY It's not more important. It's just coming up sooner.

JACK *(Fiddles with the dial)* Hitler's already moved into Austria. In a couple of months the whole world will be in it . . . What's the matter with this radio? *(It is barely audible)*

KATE *(Comes out of the kitchen)* Someone's been fooling around with it. Haven't they, Eugene?

EUGENE Why "Eugene"? Pop had the news on last night.

KATE You weren't listening to the ball game this afternoon?

JACK He's talking about Poland . . . Dammit! I don't want anyone touching this radio anymore, you understand?

EUGENE *(To the audience)* Guess who's gonna get blamed for the war in Europe?

KATE   Eugene! Bring in the knives and forks.
(*He does.* JACK *turns off the radio*)

STANLEY   You really think there'll be war, Pop? I mean, America too?

JACK   We're already in it. Not us maybe. But friends, relatives. If you're Jewish, you've got a cousin suffering *somewhere* in the world.

KATE (*Wiping the table*)   Ida Kazinsky's family got out of Poland last month. The stories she tells about what's going on there, you don't even want to hear.

STANLEY   How many relatives do we have in Europe?

KATE   Enough. Uncles, cousins. I have a great-aunt. Your father has nephews.

JACK   I have a cousin, Sholem, in Poland. His whole family.

BLANCHE   Dave had relatives in Warsaw. That's where his mother was born.

STANLEY   What if they got to America? Where would they live?

JACK   Who?

STANLEY   Your nephews. Mom's cousins and uncles. Would we take them in?

JACK (*Looks at* KATE)   What God gives us to deal with, we deal with.

STANLEY   Where would we put them?

KATE   What are you worrying about things like that now for? Go upstairs and work on your speech.

STANLEY   What speech?

KATE   How you're going to ask Mr. Stroheim for a raise tomorrow.

STANLEY   (*Looks apprehensively at* EUGENE)   Can I talk to you later, Pop? After you've rested and read your paper?

EUGENE   (*Has taken part of his father's paper, opens it*)   Lou Gehrig got two hits today. Larrupin Lou is hitting three-oh-two!

KATE   (*Grabs the paper away*)   Is that your paper? How many times have I told you you don't read it until your father is finished?

EUGENE   I didn't break it. The print doesn't come off if I take a quick look at it.

JACK   Don't be fresh to your mother. Upstairs.

STANLEY   Pop?

JACK   Everybody.

STANLEY   I'll come down later, okay, Pop?

EUGENE   C'mon, Stan. I have to talk to you anyway.
         (*They start toward the stairs*)

STANLEY   (*To* EUGENE)   You're a pest! Did anyone ever tell you you're a pest?

EUGENE   Yeah. I have a list upstairs. You wanna add your name to it?
(He taps STANLEY *on the forehead with his forefinger. It is annoying and* STAN *chases him up the stairs)*

KATE *(To* JACK*)*   Maybe you should lie down. There's nothing in that paper that's going to cheer you up.

JACK *(Thoughtfully)*   What *would* we do, Kate? Where would we put them if they got off the boat and knocked on our door? How would we feed them?

KATE   The boat didn't get here yet. I can't deal with boats that haven't landed yet.
(NORA *bursts out of the kitchen, apparently having just argued with her mother. She is followed by* BLANCHE *and* LAURIE*)*

NORA *(Determined)*   Uncle Jack! I know you're tired and you have a lot of things on your mind, but the rest of my life may depend on your decision and I have to know tonight because I have to call Mr. Beckman and let him know if I can go or not.

JACK   Who's Mr. Beckman?

NORA   The Broadway producer we talked about at dinner.

LAURIE   *Abracadabra*? Remember?
(We see STANLEY *walk to the bathroom—*EUGENE *walks into the bedroom)*

BLANCHE   Laurie! Upstairs! This minute . . . Nora, not now. This isn't the time.

NORA *(Angrily)*   It's *never* the time. You won't make a decision and I don't have anyone else I can talk to.

Well, I'll make my own decision if no one else is interested. I'm sixteen and a half years old and I'll do what I *want* to do.

(The tears begin to flow as she runs out the front door to the yard)

JACK   What is this all about?

KATE   Go on out, Jack. Talk to her.

BLANCHE   I'll take care of it. Nora's right. It's my decision.

KATE   What are you going to tell her? That she can leave school? That she can throw her future away? Is that what you want to do?

BLANCHE   What if I'm wrong? What if she's got talent? What is it I'm *supposed* to say?

JACK   She can't talk to me? It's all the same family, isn't it? I'm her uncle, for God's sake.

KATE   She doesn't need an uncle tonight. She needs a father . . . Go on. She'll tell you.

(JACK looks at them both, then walks out to the front yard. NORA is sitting on the bench, tearfully)

BLANCHE   I never learned . . .

JACK *(To* NORA*)*   You mind if I sit with you?

BLANCHE   I wrapped my life up in Dave so much, I never learned to be their mother.

JACK   If you want to talk, we'll talk; if not, not.

KATE   We have enough mothers here. This is a family. The world doesn't survive without families . . . Laurie, do your homework. Blanche, make me some tea. You're the only one here who makes decent tea.

> (LAURIE *goes up to her room.* BLANCHE *and* KATE *have gone into the kitchen*)

JACK   Listen . . . I know what it's like, Nora. Not to be heard.

NORA   You do?

JACK   I grew up in a family of four children. My father, before he died, never could remember our names. My oldest brother was "the big one," I was "the little one." My brother Sol was "the rotten one," Eddie was "the skinny one."

NORA   Who am I?

JACK   The pretty one . . . What's the problem?
> (STANLEY *walks from the bathroom, into the bedroom*)

NORA   I don't know. It doesn't seem very important now.

JACK   I've never seen you cry over something that wasn't important. I know I'm not your father. It's not my place to make decisions for you. But I can offer advice. Advice is free. If it doesn't fit, you can always return it.

NORA   Can we walk down the block?

JACK   Sure. We'll take a look at the ocean. My father always used to say, "Throw your problems out to sea and the answers will wash back up on the shore."

NORA   Did they?

JACK   Not in Brighton Beach. Orange peels and water-melon pits washed up. That's why it's good to take someone who knows how to give advice.
(She gets up and they walk off toward the beach.

STANLEY is lying on his bed, hands under his head, deep in thought. EUGENE sits on his bed, banging a baseball into his glove)

STANLEY   Will you stop that? I'm trying to think.

EUGENE   I'm glad I don't have your problems.

STANLEY   How'd you like an official American League baseball in your mouth?

EUGENE   I've got to talk to you, Stanley. I mean a really serious, important talk.

STANLEY   Everybody in this house has to have a talk with somebody. Take a number off the wall and wait your turn.

EUGENE   I had a dream last night. It was about this girl. I can't tell you her name but she's gorgeous. We were really kissing hard and rubbing up against each other and I felt this tremendous build-up coming like at the end of *The Thirty-nine Steps*. And suddenly there was an explosion. Like a dam broke and everything rushed and flowed out to sea. It was the greatest feeling I ever had in my life . . . and when I woke up, I was—I was—

STANLEY   All wet.

EUGENE (*Surprised*)   Yeah! How'd you know?

STANLEY (*Unimpressed*)   It was a wet dream. You had a wet dream. I have them all the time.

EUGENE   You do? You mean there's nothing wrong with you if it happens?

STANLEY   You never had one before?

EUGENE   Yeah, but I slept through it.

STANLEY   Didn't you ever try to do it by yourself?

EUGENE   What do you mean?

STANLEY   Didn't you ever diddle with yourself?

EUGENE   No. Never.

STANLEY   Baloney. I've heard you. You diddle three, four times a week.

EUGENE   You're crazy! What do you mean, diddle?

STANLEY   Whack off. Masturbate.

EUGENE   Will you be quiet! Laurie might hear you.

STANLEY   There's nothing wrong with it. Everybody does it. Especially at our age. It's natural.

EUGENE   What do you mean, everybody? You know guys who do it?

STANLEY Every guy I know does it. Except Haskell Fleischmann, the fat kid. He does it to the other guys.

EUGENE I can't believe I'm having this conversation.

STANLEY You can't grow up without doing it. Your voice won't change.

EUGENE Where do you get this stuff from? Is it in a medical book or something?

STANLEY It's puberty.

EUGENE It's what?

STANLEY Puberty. You never heard that word before? You don't read books?

EUGENE Yeah. *The Citadel* by A. J. Cronin. He never mentioned puberty.

STANLEY Even Pop did it.

EUGENE Pop? *Our* pop? You know what, Stanley? I think you're full of shit.

STANLEY (*Sits up*) Hey! Don't you use that language. Who do you think you are? You're just a kid. Never let me hear you say that word again.

EUGENE I don't get you. You mean it's okay for you to say "puberty" but I can't say "shit"?

STANLEY "Puberty" is a scientific word. "Shit" is for those guys who hang around the beach.

EUGENE What do you expect me to say when you tell me that Pop whacks off?

STANLEY   I don't mean he still does it, because he's married now. But when he was a kid. Fourteen or fifteen. The whole world whacks off.

EUGENE   President Roosevelt too?

STANLEY   Rich kids are the worst. They whack off from morning till night. In college, they sit around in their dorms drinking beer and whacking off.

EUGENE   Stanley, this is the most useful information you ever taught me . . . What about girls?

STANLEY   Five times as much as boys.

EUGENE   *Five* times as much? Is that an actual figure? Where do you know all this from?

STANLEY   You pick it up. You learn it. It's handed down from generation to generation. That's how our culture spreads.

EUGENE   Five times as much as boys? Some of them don't even say hello to you and they're home all night whacking off.

STANLEY   They're human just like we are. They have the same needs and desires.

EUGENE   Then why is it so hard to touch their boobs?

STANLEY   If you were a girl, would you like some guy jumping at you and grabbing your boobs?

EUGENE   If I had boobs, I would love to touch them, wouldn't you?

STANLEY   I've got my own problems to think about.

EUGENE   How do girls do it?

STANLEY   I can't explain it.

EUGENE   Please, Stanley. I'll be your slave for a month. Tell me how they do it.

STANLEY   I need a pencil and paper. I'll do it later.

EUGENE (*Quickly hands him his notebook and a pencil*)   Do you want crayons? Maybe you should do it in color?

STANLEY   Hey, Eugene. I have a major problem in my life. I haven't got time to draw girls masturbating for you.

EUGENE   I'll bet Nora doesn't do it.

STANLEY   Boy, could I win money from you. You think she's in the bathroom seven times a day just taking showers?

EUGENE   She does it in the bathroom?

STANLEY   I knew two girls who used to do it in English class. I saw a girl do it during a final exam and she got a ninety-eight on her paper . . . Is she the one you were thinking about last night?

EUGENE   No. It was somebody else. One of the beach girls.

STANLEY   It was Nora. I see what's going on. I knew why you dropped your napkin twelve times at dinner tonight.

EUGENE   She drives me crazy. I think I'm in love with her.

STANLEY   Yeah? Well, forget it. She's your cousin.

EUGENE   What's wrong with being in love with your cousin?

STANLEY   Because it's against the laws of nature. If she was your stepsister, it would be dirty, but it would be okay. But you can't love your own cousin. Let me give you a piece of advice: When you're going through puberty, don't start with anyone in your own house.

EUGENE   Who made up those rules? Franklin Roosevelt married his cousin.

STANLEY   Maybe she was his second or third cousin. But you can't marry your first cousin. You get babies with nine heads . . . I wish Pop would get back. I got to talk to him tonight.

EUGENE   I still would love to see her naked. Just once. There's nothing wrong with that, is there?

STANLEY   No. I do it all the time.

EUGENE   *You've seen Nora naked?*

STANLEY   Lots of times. I fixed the lock on the bathroom door, then opened it pretending I didn't know anyone was in there.

EUGENE   I can't believe it. What a pig! . . . What did she look like?

STANLEY   All I can tell you is I was pretty miserable she was my first cousin.
      (*He lies back on his bed.* EUGENE *turns and looks out at the audience*)

59

EUGENE   That was the night I discovered lust and guilt were very closely related. *(To* STANLEY*)* I have to wash up.

STANLEY *(Teasingly)*   Have a good time.

EUGENE   I don't do that.
    (BLANCHE *and* KATE *come out of the kitchen. They each have a cup of tea. They sit at the dining table)*

KATE   I'm sorry. I forgot it was this Tuesday. I'll change my doctor appointment.

BLANCHE   You don't have to change anything. The girls will be with me.

KATE   Have I ever missed a year going to the grave? Dave was my favorite in the whole family, you know that.

BLANCHE   You realize it'll be six years? Sometimes I forget his birthday, but the day he died I never forget.

KATE   There wasn't another one like him.

BLANCHE   Laurie asks me questions about him all the time. Was he funny? What was the funniest thing he ever said, she asked me. I couldn't remember. Isn't that awful, Kate?

KATE   Sometimes you talk like your life is over. You're still a young woman. You're still beautiful, if you'd ever stop squinting so much.

BLANCHE   I went with him for two years before we were married. What was I waiting for? That's two married years I didn't have with him.

KATE   Listen. Jack's company is having their annual affair in New York next Wednesday. At the Commodore Hotel. You should see how some of those women get dressed up. Jack wants you to come with us. He told me to ask you.

BLANCHE   Me? Who do I know in Jack's company?

KATE   You'll be with *us*. You'll meet people. Max Green'll be at our table. He's the one whose wife died last year from *(He whispers)*—tuberculosis . . . He's their number one salesman. He lives in a hotel on the Grand Concourse. He's a riot. You'll like him. Maybe you'll dance with him. What else are you going to do here every night?

BLANCHE   I don't have a dress to wear for a thing like that.

KATE   You'll make something. Jack'll get you some material. He knows everybody in the garment district.

BLANCHE   Thank you, Kate. I appreciate it. I can't go. Maybe next year.

KATE   Next year you won't have any eyes altogether. What are you afraid of, Blanche? Dave is dead. You're not. If God wanted the both of you, you'd be laying in the grave next to him.

BLANCHE   I've made plans for next Wednesday night.

KATE   More important than this? They have this affair once a year.

BLANCHE   I'm having dinner with someone.

KATE   You're having dinner? With a man? That's wonderful. Why didn't you tell me?

BLANCHE   With Mr. Murphy.
(*This stops* KATE *right in her tracks*)

KATE   Who's Mr. Murphy? . . . Oh, my God! I don't understand you. You're going to dinner with that man? Do you know where he'll take you? To a saloon. To a Bar and Grill, that's where he'll take you.

BLANCHE   We're going to Chardov's, the Hungarian restaurant. You never even met the man, why do you dislike him so much?

KATE   I don't have to meet that kind. I just have to smell his breath when he opens the window. What do you think a man like that is looking for? I grew up with that kind on Avenue A. How many times have Stanley and Gene come home from school black and blue from the beatings they took from those Irish hooligans? What have you got to talk to with a man like that?

BLANCHE   Is that why you don't like him? Because he's Irish? When have the Jews and the Irish ever fought a war? You know who George Bernard Shaw is?

KATE   I don't care who he is.

BLANCHE   One of the greatest Irish writers in the world? What would you say if *he* took me to Chardov's next Wednesday?

KATE   Is Mr. Murphy a writer? Tell him to bring me some of his books, I'll be glad to read them.

BLANCHE   Kate, when are you going to give up being an older sister?

KATE   I've heard stories about him. With women. They like their women, you know. Well, if that's what you want, it's your business.

EUGENE *(To the audience)*   I decided to go downstairs and quiet my passion with oatmeal cookies.

BLANCHE   We took a walk along the beach last Thursday. He hardly said a word. He's very shy. Very quiet. He told me where his parents came from in Ireland. Their life wasn't any easier than Momma and Poppa's in Russia.

KATE   *Nobody* had it like they had it in Russia.

BLANCHE   He holds down a decent job in a printers' office and he didn't smell of liquor and he behaved like a perfect gentleman.
   (EUGENE *comes down the stairs. He had been listening*)

KATE *(Without turning)*   No cookies for you. Not until you eat that liver.

EUGENE   You're still saving it? You mean it's going to be in the icebox until I grow up?

KATE   No cookies, you hear me?

EUGENE   I just want a glass of water.

KATE   You have water in your bathroom.

EUGENE   There's toothpaste in the glass. It makes me nauseous.
   (He goes into the kitchen)

KATE *(To* BLANCHE *)*   Listen, there's no point discussing this. I'm going to bed. Do what you want.

BLANCHE   Kate! . . . I don't want to do anything that's going to make you unhappy. Or Jack. I owe too much to you. I can't live off you the rest of my life. Every decent job I've tried to get, they turn me down because of my eyes. The thought of marrying Frank Murphy hasn't even occurred to me. Maybe not even to him. But I don't think one dinner at Chardov's is the end of the world.

KATE   I just don't want to see you get hurt. I never mean you harm. I can take anything except when someone in the family is mad at me.

BLANCHE *(Embraces her)*   I could never be mad at you, Kate. That I promise you to my dying day.

KATE   Go on. Have dinner with Frank Murphy. If Poppa ever heard me say those words, he'd get up from the cemetery and stand in front of our house with a big stick.
   *(*BLANCHE *kisses her again)*

BLANCHE   I told him to pick me up here. Is that all right?

KATE   *Here?* In *my* house?

BLANCHE   For two minutes. I wanted you to meet him. At least see what he's like.

KATE   Tell his mother to wash her windows, maybe I'd know what he's like.
(*We see* NORA *hurriedly cross the front yard and open the front door. She looks upset.* NORA *walks over to her mother, determined*)

NORA   Can I see Mr. Beckman tomorrow? Yes or no?
(JACK *crosses the front yard*)

BLANCHE   Did you talk to Uncle Jack?

NORA   I talked to Uncle Jack. I want an answer from *you*, Mother. Yes or no?
(JACK *enters the house*)

BLANCHE   What did he say?

NORA   It doesn't matter what he said. It's your decision or mine. Who's going to make it, Mother?

JACK   I said if I were her father, I'd tell her to finish high school. If she's got talent, there'll be plenty of other shows. I never got past the eighth grade and that's why I spend half my life on the subway and the other half trying to make a few extra dollars to keep this family from being out on the street.

NORA   (*To* BLANCHE)   I don't want this just for myself, Momma, but for you and for Laurie. In a few years we could have a house of our own, instead of all being cooped up here like animals. We could pay Uncle Jack for what he's given us all these years. I'm asking for a way out, Momma. Don't shut me in. Don't shut me in for the rest of my life.
(*They all turn and look at* BLANCHE)

65

BLANCHE   You promised you'd do what Uncle Jack said.

NORA   He doesn't make decisions—he offers advice. I want a decision, Momma. From you . . . Please!

BLANCHE   You finish high school. You tell Mr. Beckman you're too young. You tell him your mother said "No" . . . That's my decision.

NORA *(Looks at her, frustrated)*   I see. *(To* JACK*)* Thank you very much, Uncle Jack, for your advice. *(To* BLANCHE*)*   I'll let you know in the morning what *my* decision is.
   (She rushes upstairs to her room. BLANCHE *starts to go after her)*

KATE   Let her go, Blanche. Let her sleep on it. You'll only make it worse.

BLANCHE   It seems no matter *what* I do, I only make it worse.
   (She turns, starts up the stairs.
   NORA *has slammed the door of her room.* STANLEY *hears it and opens his door and starts down)*

JACK *(To* KATE*)*   What could I tell her? What could I say?

KATE *(Shrugs)*   You inherit a family, you inherit their problems.

EUGENE *(Comes out of the kitchen)*   Well, good night.

KATE   Put the cookie on the table.

EUGENE   What cookie?

KATE   The oatmeal cookie in your pocket. Put it on the table.

EUGENE   You can smell an oatmeal cookie from ten feet
away?

KATE   I heard the jar moving in the kitchen. Suddenly
everybody's doing what they want in this house. Your
father's upset, Aunt Blanche is upset, *put the cookie on
that table*!
    (EUGENE *puts the cookie on the table and starts up the
    stairs to his room. He passes* STANLEY)

STANLEY (*To* EUGENE)   I heard a lot of yelling. What
happened?

EUGENE   I don't know, but it's my fault.
    (*He goes on up and into the bathroom.*
        NORA *is on her bed, crying.* LAURIE *sits on her bed
    and watches her*)

LAURIE   What are you going to do?   (NORA *shakes her
    head, indicating she doesn't know*)   Do you want *me* to
    speak to Mom? I could tell her I was getting flutters in
    my heart again.

NORA (*Turns, angrily*)   Don't you ever say that! Don't
you pretend to be sick to get favors from anyone.

LAURIE   I'm not pretending. They're just not *big* flutters.
    (STANLEY *has been sitting at the top of the stairs
    trying to work up courage to talk to his father.*

    JACK *is sitting in the living room, disconsolate.* KATE
    is puffing up pillows)

JACK   Stop puffing up pillows. The house could be burn-
ing down and you'd run back in to puff up the pillows.

KATE   Let's go to bed. You're tired.

JACK   When does it get easier, Kate? When does our life get easier?

KATE   At night. When you get seven good hours of sleep. That's the easiest it ever gets.
(NORA *has put on her robe, left her room and opens the bathroom door. We hear a scream from* EUGENE)

EUGENE   *CLOSE THE DOOR!!!*

NORA   Oh. I'm sorry. I didn't know anyone was in there. *(She rushes out, back to her room.*
STANLEY *moves into the living room)*

STANLEY   Dad? Do you think I could talk to you now? It'll just take five minutes.

KATE   He's tired, Stanley. He's practically asleep.

STANLEY   Two minutes. I'll tell it as fast as I can.

JACK   Go on, Kate. Go to bed. The boy wants to tell me something.

KATE   Turn out the lights when you're through. *(She kisses* JACK's *head)* Don't worry about things. We've always made them work out.
(She leaves the room just as EUGENE *darts out of the bathroom, rushes into his own room and slams the door)*

EUGENE   She saw me on the crapper! Nora saw me on the crapper! *(He falls on his bed)* I might as well be dead.

STANLEY   I have a problem, Pop.

JACK   If you didn't, you wouldn't live in this house.

68

STANLEY It must be tough being a father. Everybody comes to you with their problems. You have to have all the answers. I don't know if *I* could handle it.

JACK Stop trying to win me over. Just tell me the problem.

STANLEY I got fired today!

JACK *What???*

STANLEY Don't get excited! Don't get crazy! Let me explain what happened.

JACK What did you do? You came in late? You were fresh to somebody? Were you fresh to somebody?

STANLEY I'm not fired yet. I can still get my job back. I just need you to help me make a decision.

JACK Take the job back. I don't care what it is. This is *not* the time for anybody to be out of work in this family.

STANLEY When I was twelve years old you gave me a talk about principles. Remember?

JACK All night you waited to tell me this news?

STANLEY This is about principles, Pop.

JACK How long were you going to go without telling me?

STANLEY Will you at least hear my principles?

JACK All right, I'll hear your principles. Then you'll hear mine.

STANLEY   Just sit back and let me tell you what happened. Okay? Well, it was on account of Andrew, the colored guy who sweeps up.

(JACK *sits back and listens.* STANLEY *sits with his back to the audience, talking, but we can't hear him. Our attention is drawn to* EUGENE *up in his room*)

EUGENE (*To the audience*)   . . . So Stanley began his sad story. Pop never said a word. He just sat there and listened. Stanley was terrific. It was like that movie, *Abe Lincoln in Illinois.* Stanley was not only defending his principles, he was defending democracy and the United States of America. Pop must have been bleary-eyed because not only did he have to deal with Stanley's principles, Nora's career, the loss of his noisemaker business, how to get Aunt Blanche married off and Laurie's fluttering heart, but at any minute there could be a knock on the door with thirty-seven relatives from Poland showing up looking for a place to live . . . Finally, Stanley finished his story.

STANLEY   So—either I bring in a letter of apology in the morning or I don't bother coming in . . . I know it's late. I know you're tired. But I didn't want to do anything without asking you first.

JACK (*After a few moments of silence*)   Ohh, Stanley, Stanley, Stanley!

STANLEY   I'm sorry, Pop.

JACK   You shouldn't have swept the dirt on his shoes.

STANLEY   I know.

JACK   Especially in front of other people.

STANLEY   I know.

JACK   He's your boss. He pays your salary. His money helps put food on our dining table.

STANLEY   I know, Pop.

JACK   And we don't have money to waste. Believe me when I tell you that.

STANLEY   I believe you, Pop.

JACK   You were sick three days last year and he only docked you a day and a half's pay, remember that?

STANLEY   I know. I can see what you're getting at. I'll write the letter. I'll do it tonight.

JACK   On the other hand, you did a courageous thing. You defended a fellow worker. Nobody else stood up for him, did they?

STANLEY   I was the only one.

JACK   That's something to be proud of. It was what you believed in. That's standing up for your principles.

STANLEY   That's why I didn't want to write the letter. I knew you'd understand.

JACK   The question is, Can this family afford principles right now?

STANLEY   It would make it hard, I know.

JACK   Not just on you and me. But on your mother. On Aunt Blanche, Nora, Laurie.

STANLEY   Eugene.

JACK   Eugene. Eugene would have to get a part-time job. Time he should be using studying books to get himself somewhere.

STANLEY   He wants to be a writer. He wants to go to college.

JACK   I wish I could have sent *you*. I've always been sick about that, Stanley.

STANLEY   I like working, Pop. I really do . . . Listen, I made up my mind. I'm going to write the letter.

JACK   I'm not saying you should . . .

STANLEY   I know. It's *my* decision. I really want to write the letter.

JACK   And how will your principles feel in the morning?

STANLEY   My principles feel better already. You told me you were proud of what I did. That's all I really cared about.

JACK   You know something, Stanley—I don't think there's much in college they could teach you that you don't already know.

STANLEY   Guess who I learned it from? . . . Thanks for talking to me, Pop. See you in the morning. You coming to bed?

JACK   I think I'll sit here for a while. It's the only time of day I have a few minutes to myself.

(STANLEY *nods, then bounds up the stairs to his room.* JACK *sits back in his chair and closes his eyes.*

STANLEY *enters his room.* EUGENE *is writing in his book of memoirs)*

EUGENE   How'd it go? Do you have to write the letter?

STANLEY   Yeah.
(*He gets out a pad and his fountain pen*)

EUGENE   I *knew* that's what he'd make you do.

STANLEY   He didn't *make* me do it . . . Be quiet, will ya! I have to concentrate.

EUGENE   What are you going to say?

STANLEY   I don't know . . . You want to help me? You're good at those things.

EUGENE   People used to get paid for that in the old days. Professional letter writers.

STANLEY (*Indignant*)   I'm not going to pay you money.

EUGENE   I don't want money.

STANLEY   Then what *do* you want?

EUGENE   Tell me what Nora looked like naked.

STANLEY   How horny can you get?

EUGENE   I don't know. What's the highest score?

STANLEY   All right. When we finish the letter.

EUGENE   I don't trust you. I want to get paid first.

STANLEY   You know, you're a real shit!

EUGENE   Don't talk like that in front of me, I'm just a kid.

STANLEY   What do you want to know?

EUGENE   Everything. From the time you opened the door.

STANLEY   It happened so fast.

EUGENE   That's okay. Tell it slow.

STANLEY   Jesus! All right . . . I heard the shower running. I waited for it to stop. I gave a few seconds for the water to run off her body, then I knew she'd be stepping out of the shower. Suddenly I just opened the door. She was standing there on the bath mat, a towel on her head and nothing else in the whole wide world.

EUGENE   Slower. Don't go so fast.

STANLEY   Her breasts were gorgeous. Like two peaches hanging on the vine waiting to be plucked . . . Maybe nectarines. Like two nectarines, all soft and pink and shining in the morning sun . . .
                              Curtain

ACT TWO

Wednesday, a week later. About six-thirty in the evening.

KATE *comes down the stairs carrying a tray of food. She looks a little haggard.*

LAURIE *is lying on the sofa in the living room with a book.*

EUGENE *is in the backyard, sitting on the beach chair, writing in his book of memoirs.*

KATE   Laurie! You should see your mother. She looks gorgeous.

LAURIE   I'm waiting for her grand entrance . . . How's Uncle Jack?

KATE   He's resting. He ate a nice dinner. You can go up and see him later. *(She yells)* Eugene! Your father's resting. I don't want to hear any ball playing against the wall.

EUGENE   I'm not playing. I'm writing.

KATE   Well, do it quietly.
(She goes into the kitchen)

EUGENE *(To the audience)*   She wants me to write quietly. If that was the only sentence I published in my memoirs, it would be a best seller . . . Everybody's been in a rotten mood around here lately . . . Three days ago Pop had a *(He whispers)*—heart attack. It wasn't a major *(He whispers)*—heart attack. It was sort of a warning. He passed out in the subway and a policeman had to bring him home. He was trying to make extra money driving a cab at nights and he just plain wore out . . . The doctor says he has to stay home for two or three weeks, but Pop won't listen to him. Mr. Jacobson has a brother-in-law who needs a job. He's filling in for Pop temporarily, but Pop's afraid that three weeks in bed could turn into permanently.

(STANLEY *appears, coming home from work. He looks distraught. He half whispers to* EUGENE)

STANLEY I have to talk to you.

EUGENE What's up?

STANLEY Not here. In our room. Don't tell anybody.

EUGENE What's the big secret?

STANLEY Will you shut up! Wait'll I get upstairs, then follow me.
(*He goes into the house*)

EUGENE If it's about Nora, I'm not interested. (*To the audience*) I forgot to tell you, I hate my cousin Nora. She's been real snotty to everybody lately. She doesn't say hello in the morning and eats her dinner up in her room. And she's been seeing this guy Larry No Chin Clurman every night. And she's not as pretty as I thought she was . . .

KATE (*Walking out of the kitchen*) Eugene! Did you bring your father his paper?

EUGENE I'm coming. My knee hurts. I fell down the stairs at school.

KATE Well, bring it up. Your father's waiting for it.
(*She goes back into the kitchen*)

EUGENE (*To the audience*) If I told her I just lost both my hands in an accident she'd say, "Go upstairs and wash your face with your feet" . . . I guess she's sore because she and Pop can't go to the affair at the Commodore Hotel. They had Glen Gray and his orchestra . . . I feel sorry for her 'cause she doesn't get to go out much. (*He gets up, starts toward the house*) And she's nervous about Frank Murphy coming over to pick up Aunt Blanche. She's angry at the whole world. (*He enters the house*) That's why she's making lima beans for dinner.

KATE (*Walks into the living room with a dish of nuts*) Would you like a cashew, Laurie?

LAURIE   Oh, thanks. (*She takes one*) And a Brazil nut too? (*She takes one*) And one almond? (*She takes one*)

KATE   You must be starved. We're having dinner late tonight. We'll wait till your mother goes out.

EUGENE (*Limps into the living room*)   Can I have some nuts, Mom?

KATE   Just one. It's for the company.   (*He takes one, starts upstairs*)   We're eating in the kitchen tonight. You and Stanley help with the dishes.
        (*He goes upstairs*)

KATE (*To* LAURIE)   You look all flushed. You don't have a fever, do you? (*She feels* LAURIE*'s head*) Let me see your tongue. (LAURIE *shows her her tongue*) It's all spotted.

LAURIE   That's the cashew nut.

KATE   Don't you get sick on me too. If you're tired, I want you in bed.

LAURIE   I have a little stomach cramp. Maybe I'm getting my "ladies."

KATE   Your what?

LAURIE   My "ladies." That thing that Nora gets when she can't go in the water.

KATE   I don't think so. Not at your age. But if your stomach hurts real bad, you come and tell me. I made a nice tuna fish salad tonight. Call me when your mother comes down.
   (*She starts toward the kitchen*)

LAURIE   Aunt Kate! . . . Does Momma like Mr. Murphy?

KATE   I don't know, darling. I don't think she knows him very well yet.

LAURIE   Do you like him?

KATE   I never spoke to the man.

LAURIE   You called him a Cossack. Are those the kind who don't like Jewish people?

KATE   I'm sure Mr. Murphy likes your mother, otherwise he wouldn't be taking her out to dinner.

LAURIE   If Mom married him, would we have to live in that dark house across the street? With that creepy woman in the window?

KATE   We're not up to that yet. Let's just get through Chardov's Restaurant first.
   (*She goes into the kitchen.*
   EUGENE *rushes into his room.* STANLEY *is lying on his bed, hands under his head, staring at the ceiling*)

EUGENE   Pop's feeling better. He threw the newspaper at me because I didn't bring him the evening edition.

STANLEY *(Sits up)*   Lock the door.

EUGENE *(Locking the door)*   You look terrible. You were crying. Your eyes are all red.

STANLEY   I'm in trouble, Eug. I mean, real, *real* trouble. *(He takes a single cigarette out of his shirt pocket, puts it in his mouth and lights it with a match)*

EUGENE   When did you take up smoking?

STANLEY   I smoke in the stockroom all the time. Don't let me see you do it. It's a bad habit.

EUGENE   So how come *you* do it?

STANLEY   I like it.

EUGENE   What brand do you smoke?

STANLEY   Lucky Strikes.

EUGENE   I knew you would. That's the best brand.

STANLEY   Swear to God, what I tell you, you'll never tell a living soul.

EUGENE *(Raises his hand)*   I take an oath on the life of the entire New York Yankees . . . What happened?

STANLEY *(He paces before he can speak)*   . . . I lost my salary.

EUGENE   *What?*

STANLEY   The entire seventeen dollars. It's gone. I lost it.

EUGENE   Where? In the subway?

STANLEY   In a poker game. I lost it gambling.

EUGENE   IN A POKER GAME?

STANLEY   *Will you shut up??* You want to kill Pop right in his bedroom?

EUGENE   You never told me you gambled.

STANLEY   We would just do it at lunch hour. For pennies. I always won. A dime. A quarter. It wasn't just luck. I was really good.

EUGENE   Seventeen dollars!!

STANLEY   When Pop got sick, I thought I could make some extra money. To help out. So I played in this game over in the stockroom at Florsheim Shoes . . . Boy, did I learn about poker. They cleaned me out in twenty minutes . . .

EUGENE   What are you going to tell them?

STANLEY   I don't know. If Pop wasn't sick, I would tell him the truth. Last week he tells me how proud he is of me. He's driving a cab at nights and I'm playing poker at Florsheim's.
  (He puts his head down and starts to cry)

EUGENE   Yeah, but suppose you won? Suppose you won fifty dollars? You just had bad luck, that's all.

STANLEY   I had no chance against those guys. They were gamblers. They all wore black pointy shoes with clocks on their socks . . . If Pop dies, I'll hang myself, I swear.

EUGENE   Don't talk like that. Pop isn't going to die. He ate three lamb chops tonight . . . Why don't you just say you lost the money? You had a hole in your pocket. You can tear a hole in your pocket.

STANLEY   I already used that one.

EUGENE   When?

STANLEY   In November when I lost five dollars. He said to me, "From now on, check your pockets every morning."

EUGENE   What happened to the five dollars? Did you gamble that too?

STANLEY   No. I gave it to a girl . . . You know. A pro.

EUGENE   A pro what? . . . A PROSTITUTE??? You went to one of those places? Holy shit!

STANLEY   I'm not going to warn you about that word again.

EUGENE   Is that what it costs? Five dollars?

STANLEY   Two-fifty. I went with this guy I know. He still owes me.

EUGENE   And you never told me? What was she like? Was she pretty? How old was she?

STANLEY   Don't start in with me, Eugene.

EUGENE   Did she get completely naked or what?

STANLEY (*Furious*)   Every time I get in trouble, I have to tell you what a naked girl looks like? . . . Do me a favor, Eugene. Go in the bathroom, whack off and grow up by yourself.

EUGENE   Don't get sore. If you were me, you'd ask the same questions.

STANLEY   Well, I never had an older brother to teach me those things. I had to do it all on my own. You don't know how lucky you are to be the younger one. You don't have the responsibilities I do. You're still in school looking up girls' dresses on the staircase.

EUGENE   I work plenty hard in school.

STANLEY   Yeah? Well, let me see your report card. Today's the first of the month, I know you got it. I want to see your report card.

EUGENE   I don't have to show you my report card. You're not my father.

STANLEY   Yes, I am. As long as Pop is sick, I am. I'm the only one in the family who's working, ain't I?

EUGENE   Really? Well, where's your salary this week, Pop?

STANLEY   (*Grabs* EUGENE *in anger*)   I hate you sometimes. You're nothing but a lousy shit. I help you all the time and you never help me without wanting something for it. I hate your disgusting guts.

EUGENE   (*Screaming*)   Not as much as I hate yours. You snore at night. You pick your toenails. You smell up the bathroom. When I go in there I have to puke.

STANLEY   (*Screaming back*)   Give me your report card. Give it to me, goddammit, or I'll beat your face in.

EUGENE *(Starts to cry)*   You want it? Here! *(He grabs it out of a book)* Here's my lousy report card . . . you fuck!!

> *(He falls on the bed crying, his face to the wall.* STANLEY *sits on his own bed and reads the report card. There is a long silence)*

STANLEY *(Softly)*   Four A's and a B . . . That's good. That's real good, Eugene . . . You're smart . . . I want you to go to college . . . I want you to be somebody important someday . . . Because I'm not . . . I'm no damn good. *(He is crying)* I'm sorry I said those things to you.

EUGENE *(Still faces the wall. It's too hard to look at* STAN*)* Me too . . . I'm sorry too.

> *(*JACK *appears at the top of the stairs. He is in his pajamas, robe and slippers. He seems very shaky. He holds on to the banister and slowly comes down the stairs.*
>
> *He looks around, then sees* LAURIE *and walks into the living room. His breath does not come easy)*

LAURIE *(Sees him)*   Hi, Uncle Jack. Are you feeling better?

JACK   A little, darling. Your mother's not down yet?

LAURIE   No.

JACK   I wanted to see her before she goes out.
> *(*KATE *comes out of the kitchen with a bowl of fruit. She sees* JACK*)*

KATE   Oh, my God! Are you crazy? Are you out of your mind? You're walking down the stairs?

JACK I'm all right. I was tired lying in that bed. I wanted to see Blanche.

(*He sits down slowly*)

KATE How are you going to get upstairs? You think I'm going to carry you? The doctor said you're not even supposed to go to the bathroom, didn't he?

JACK You trust doctors? My grandmother never saw one in her life, she lived to be eighty-seven.

KATE She didn't have high blood pressure. She never fainted on the subway.

JACK She used to faint three, four times a week. It's in our family. We're fainters. Laurie, darling, go get your Uncle Jack a glass of ice water, please.

LAURIE Now?

JACK Yes. Now, sweetheart. (LAURIE *gets up and goes into kitchen*) That child is pampered too much. You should let her do more work around the house. You don't get healthy lying on couches all day.

KATE No. You get healthy driving cabs at night after you work nine hours cutting raincoats. You want to kill yourself, Jack? You want to leave me to take care of this family alone? Is that what you want?

JACK You figure I'll get better faster if you make me feel guilty? . . . I was born with enough guilt, Katey. If I need more, I'll ask you.

KATE I'm sorry. You know me. I'm not happy unless I can worry. *My* family were worriers. Worriers generally marry fainters.

JACK *(Takes her hand, holds it)*   I'm not going to leave you. I promise. If I didn't leave you for another woman, I'm certainly not going to drop dead just to leave you.

KATE *(Lets go of his hand)*   What other woman? That bookkeeper, Helene?

JACK   Again with Helene? You're never going to forget that I danced with her two years in a row at the Commodore Hotel?

KATE   Don't tell me she isn't attracted to you. I noticed that right off.

JACK   What does a woman like that want with a cutter? She likes the men up front. The salesmen. She's a widow. She's looking to get married.

KATE   You're an attractive man, Jack. Women like you.

JACK   Me? Attractive? You really must think I'm dying, don't you?

KATE   You don't know women like I do. Just promise me one thing. If anything ever happened with you and that Helene, let me go to my grave without hearing it.

JACK   I see. Now that you're worried about Helene, you've decided you're going to die first.
        (LAURIE *comes back in with a glass of ice water*)

LAURIE   I had to chop the ice. I'm all out of breath.

JACK   It's good for you, darling. It's exercise.
        (*He takes the ice water.*)

        NORA *comes out of her room and goes bounding down the stairs*)

87

NORA (*Coldly*)   I'm going out. I won't be having dinner. I'll be home late. I have my key. Good night.

KATE   Nora! Don't you want to see how your mother looks?

NORA   I'm sure she looks beautiful. She doesn't need me to tell her.

KATE   What about Mr. Murphy? I know your mother wants him to meet you and Laurie. He'll be here any minute.

NORA   I have somebody waiting for me. I can meet Mr. Murphy some other time.

JACK   I think it would be nice if you waited, Nora. I think your mother would be very hurt if you didn't wait to say goodbye.

NORA   I'm sure that's very good advice, Uncle Jack. I know *just* how my mother feels. I'm not so sure she knows how *I* feel.
(*She turns and goes out the front door.* JACK *and* KATE *look at each other*)

KATE   Jack! What'll I do?

JACK   Leave it alone. It's between Nora and Blanche. It's something *they* have to work out.

KATE   Who is she going out with? Where does she go every night?

LAURIE   With Larry Clurman. He borrows his father's car and takes her to the cemetery.

KATE   What cemetery?

LAURIE   Where Daddy is buried. She goes to see Daddy.
(BLANCHE *has come out of her room and appears at the head of the stairs. She is all dressed up and looks quite lovely. She comes down the stairs*)

KATE   What'll I tell her? I don't want to spoil this evening for her.
(BLANCHE *appears in the room*)

BLANCHE   Jack? What are you doing down here?

JACK   We have company coming. Where else should I be?

BLANCHE   I looked in your room. I got scared to death.

JACK   Well, you don't look it. You look beautiful.

KATE   Ohh, Blanche. Oh, my God, Blanche, it's stunning. Like a movie star. Who's the movie star I like so much, Laurie?

LAURIE   Irene Dunne.

KATE   Like Irene Dunne.

LAURIE   I think she looks like Rosalind Russell. Maybe Carole Lombard.

JACK   I think she looks like Blanche. Blanche is prettier than all of them.

BLANCHE   I had such trouble with the make-up. I couldn't see my eyes to put on the mascara. So I had to put my glasses on. Then I couldn't get the mascara on under the glasses.
(STANLEY *gets up from his bed, goes out to the bathroom and closes the door*)

89

KATE   Where are your glasses? Have you got your glasses?

BLANCHE   In my purse. I thought I'd put them on in the restaurant, when I'm looking at the menu.

KATE   Make sure you do. I don't want you coming home telling me you don't know what he looks like.

BLANCHE   I'm so glad to see you up, Jack. Then you're feeling better?

JACK   It was nothing. I needed a rest, that's all. Besides, I wanted to meet this Murphy fella. A stranger comes in, he likes to meet another man. Makes him feel comfortable.

BLANCHE   Thank you, Jack. That's very thoughtful of you.

KATE   (*Takes something out of her pocket*)   Here. Wear this. Don't say no to me. Just put them on, Blanche. Please.

BLANCHE   Kate! Your pearls. Your good pearls.

KATE   What are they going to do? Sit in my drawer all year? Pearls are like people. They like to go out and be seen once in a while.

BLANCHE   You were going to wear them to the affair tonight. I'm so wrapped up in myself, I forgot you're missing the affair this year.

KATE   I can afford to miss it. I don't see Jack there the whole night anyway.

JACK   Let's see how they look.

BLANCHE   I'm so nervous I'll lose them.
(*She puts them on. They all look*)

KATE   All right. Tell me I don't have a beautiful sister.

JACK   Now I feel good. Now I feel I got my money's worth.

LAURIE   Definitely Carole Lombard.

BLANCHE   Laurie, go up and get Nora. I want to show them to Nora.

LAURIE   . . . She's not here. She left.

BLANCHE (*Looks at* KATE *and* JACK)   What do you mean, she left? Without saying goodbye?

KATE   She had to meet somebody. She wanted to wait for you.

BLANCHE   She could have come into my room. She knew I wanted to see her.

JACK   She'll see you when you get home. You'll look just as good at twelve o'clock.

BLANCHE   What did she say? Did she say anything?

KATE   You're going out. You're going to have a good time tonight. We'll talk about it later.

BLANCHE   She's making me pay for it, isn't she? She knows she can get to me so easily . . . That's what I get for making decisions.

JACK   I feel like ice cream for dessert. Laurie, you feel like ice cream for dessert?

LAURIE   Butter pecan?

JACK   Butter pecan for you, maple walnut for me. Go up
and tell Eugene I want him to go to the store.

LAURIE   I'll go with him.

KATE   Don't run, darling.

JACK   Let her run. If she gets tired, she'll tell you. Let's
stop worrying about each other so much.
(LAURIE *knocks on* EUGENE's *door*)

LAURIE   Eugene! Your father wants us to go to the store.

EUGENE   Tell him I'm sick. My stomach hurts.

LAURIE   You don't want any ice cream?

EUGENE (*Thinks*)   Ice cream? Wait a minute. (*He sits up,
looks out at the audience*) It's amazing how quickly you
recover from misery when someone offers you ice
cream.

JACK   She's only sixteen, Blanche. At that age they're
still wrapped up in themselves.

EUGENE   How am I going to become a writer if I
don't know how to suffer? Actually, I'd give up writing if I could see a naked girl while I was eating ice
cream.
(*He comes out of his room and goes down the stairs
with* LAURIE. STANLEY *comes out of the bathroom and
goes back into his own room*)

BLANCHE   What time is it?

KATE   Six-thirty. He'll be here any minute. Get your mind off Nora, Blanche. Don't wear my pearls out tonight for nothing.

JACK   Eugene! Go to Hanson's. Get a half pint of butter pecan, a half pint of maple walnut, a half pint of chocolate for yourself. Kate, what do you want?

KATE   I'm in no mood for ice cream.

JACK   Get her vanilla. She'll eat it. And whatever Stanley likes.

EUGENE   I need money.

JACK   I just paid the doctor fifteen dollars. Go up to Stanley. He got paid today. Ask him for his salary.

EUGENE (*In shock*)   *What???*

KATE   Here. Here's a dollar. (*She takes it out of her pocket*) Hurry back so Laurie can meet Mr. Murphy. But don't run.
   (*They take the money and leave by the front door*)

BLANCHE   You know what I worry about at night? That she'll run off. That I'll wake up in the morning and she'll be gone. To Philadelphia. Or Boston. Or God knows where.

KATE   Look how the woman's going out on a date. Is that what you're going to talk about? He'll start drinking in five minutes.

BLANCHE   You think so? What'll I do if he gets drunk?

KATE   You'll come right home. Do you have money? Do you have carfare?

BLANCHE   No. I didn't take anything.

KATE   Wait here. I'll get five dollars from Stanley. Now I have something *else* to worry about.
(She starts up the stairs)

JACK   I could use a cup of hot tea.
(He gets up)

BLANCHE   Sit there. I'll make it.

JACK   We'll both make it. Keep me company. We can hear the bell from the kitchen.
(They go off to the kitchen. KATE is at STANLEY's door. She knocks on it)

KATE   Stanley? Are you in there? *(She opens the door. STANLEY is lying on his bed)* Open the window. You never get any air in this room . . . (She extends her hand) I need five dollars for Aunt Blanche. (He stares at the floor) . . . Stanley? Did you get paid today?

STANLEY   Yes. I got paid today.

KATE   Take out your money for the week, let me have the envelope.

STANLEY *(Still stares down)*   I don't have it.

KATE   You don't have the envelope?

STANLEY   I don't have the money.

KATE   What do you mean, you don't have the money?

STANLEY   I mean I don't have the money. It's gone.

KATE *(Nervously, sits on the bed)*   It's gone? . . . Gone where?

STANLEY   It's just gone. I don't have it. I can't get it back. I'm sorry. There's nothing I can do about it anymore. Just don't ask me any more questions.

KATE   What do you mean, don't ask any more questions? I want to know what happened to seventeen dollars, Stanley!

STANLEY   You'll tell Pop. If I tell you, you're going to tell Pop.

KATE   Why shouldn't I tell your father? Why, Stanley? I want to know what happened to that money.

STANLEY   I gambled it! I lost it playing poker! All right? You happy? You satisfied now?
    (He starts to weep)

KATE *(Her breath goes out of her body. She sits there numb, then finally takes a breath)*   I'm not going to deal with this right now. I have to get Aunt Blanche out of the house first. I have your father's health to worry about. You're going to sit in this room and you're going to think up a story. You were robbed. Somebody stole the money. I don't care who, I don't care where. That's what you're going to tell your father, because if you tell him the truth, you'll kill that man as sure as I'm sitting here . . . Tonight, after he goes to sleep, you'll meet me in the kitchen and we'll deal with this alone.
    (She gets up, moves to the door)

STANLEY (*Barely audible*) . . . I'm sorry.
> (*She goes, closes the door.* STANLEY *sits there as if the life has gone out of him.*
> KATE *walks down the stairs and into the living room. She goes over to the window, looks out and breaks into sobs.*
> BLANCHE *comes out of the kitchen. She looks around the living room*)

BLANCHE   I left my purse in here. Without my glasses, I'm afraid to pour the tea. (*She notices* KATE *wiping her eyes with her handkerchief*) Kate? . . . What is it? What's wrong?

KATE   Nothing. I'm just all nerves today.

BLANCHE   You're worried about Jack. He shouldn't have come down the stairs.

KATE   He knows he's not supposed to get out of bed. What did we need a doctor for? He doesn't listen to them.

BLANCHE   I shouldn't have asked Mr. Murphy to come over. That's the only reason he came down.

KATE   It's not just Mr. Murphy. It's Stanley, it's Eugene, it's everybody.

BLANCHE   I'm sorry about Nora. Jack told me what she said when she left.

KATE   Why don't you get your purse, Blanche. He'll be here any minute.

BLANCHE   Did Nora say anything to hurt you, Kate? I know she's been very difficult these last few days.

KATE (*Suddenly turns, angrily*) Why is it always *Nora*? Why is it only *your* problems? Do you think you're the only one in this world who has troubles? We *all* have troubles. We *all* get our equal share. (*It hits* BLANCHE *like a slap in the face*)

BLANCHE I'm sorry. Forgive me, Kate. I'm sorry.

KATE Maybe you're stronger than I am, I don't know. You survived Dave's death. I don't know if I could handle it if anything happens to Jack.

BLANCHE He'll be all right, Kate. Nothing's going to happen to him. He's still a young man. He's strong.

KATE When Dave died, I cried for his loss. I was so angry. Angry at God for taking such a young man . . . I never realized until now what *you* must have gone through. How did you get through it, Blanche?

BLANCHE I had you. I had Jack . . . But mostly, you live for your children. Your children keep you going.

KATE (*Almost smiles*) My children.

BLANCHE I wake up every morning for Nora and for Laurie.

KATE Nora hurts you so much and you can still say that?

BLANCHE Why? Don't you think we hurt *our* parents? You don't remember how Momma cried when Celia left home? Sure it hurts, but if you love someone, you forgive them.

KATE   Some things you forgive. Some things you never forgive.

>   (LAURIE *comes back into the house. She has a letter in her hand*)

LAURIE   Is the ice cream here yet?

BLANCHE   No, darling. Didn't you go with Eugene?

LAURIE   No. I was across the street in the creepy house. It's just as creepy inside.

BLANCHE   In Mr. Murphy's house? You were just in there? Why?

LAURIE   She called me from the window. The old lady. I think it's his mother. She told me she had a letter for you. I had to go inside to get it.

>   (*She hands the letter to* BLANCHE)

KATE   What did she say to you?

LAURIE   She offered me a cookie but it was all green. I said I wasn't hungry.

>   (EUGENE *appears outside the house. He carries a brown paper bag with four small cartons of ice cream.* BLANCHE *opens the letter*)

EUGENE   (*To the audience*) "Dear Mrs. Morton, I send regrets for my son Frank. I tried to reach you earlier, then realized you had no phone. Frank will be unable to keep his dinner engagement with you this evening. Frank is in hospital as a result of an automobile accident last night, and although his injuries are not serious, the consequences are. As a devoted mother I would end this letter here and forward my apologies. Despite all my son's faults, honesty and sincerity have never been his failings. He wanted me to tell you the truth. That while driving a friend's motorcar, he was intoxicated and was the cause of the aforementioned accident. The truth would come out soon enough, but Frank has too much respect and fondness for you to have you hear it from some other source. I hope you will not think I am just a doting mother when I tell you my boy has a great many attributes. A great many. As soon as Frank can get out of his difficulties here we have decided to move to upstate New York where there is a clinic that can help Frank and where we have relatives with whom we can stay. Frank sends, along with his regrets, his regard for a warm, intelligent, friendly and most delightful neighbor across the way . . . Yours most respectfully, Mrs. Matthew Murphy."

KATE What is it?
(BLANCHE *hands the letter to* KATE)

BLANCHE He's not coming. He's . . . in the hospital.
(KATE *reads the letter*)

EUGENE (*To the audience*) It was a sad letter, all right, but it sure was well written. Maybe I should have been born in Ireland.
(*He walks into the house*)

KATE (*As she reads*) I knew it. I said it right from the beginning, didn't I?

LAURIE Why is he in the hospital?

BLANCHE   He was in a car accident . . . Oh, God. That poor woman.

LAURIE   Does that mean you're not going out to dinner?

KATE (*Nods her head as she finishes*)   It could have been you in that car with him. I warned you the first day about those people.

BLANCHE   Stop calling them "those people." They're not "those people." She's a mother, like you and me.

KATE   And what is he? Tell me what he is.

BLANCHE   He's somebody in trouble. He's somebody that needs help. For God's sakes, Kate, you don't even know the man.

KATE   I know the man. I know what they're *all* like.

BLANCHE   Who are you to talk? Are we any better? Are we something so special? We're *all* poor around here, the least we can be is charitable.

KATE   Why? What have *I* got I can afford to give away? Am I the one who got you all dressed up for nothing? Am I the one who got your hopes up? Am I the one they're going to lock up in a jail somewhere?

LAURIE   They're going to put him in jail?

KATE   Don't talk to me about charity. Anyone else, but not me.

BLANCHE   I never said you weren't charitable.

KATE   All I did was try to help you. All I *ever* did was try to help you.

BLANCHE   I know that. Nobody cares for their family more than you do. But at least you can be sympathetic to somebody else in trouble.

KATE   Who should I care about? Who's out there watching over *me*? I did enough in my life for people. You know what I'm talking about.

BLANCHE   No, I don't. Say what's on your mind, Kate. What people?

KATE   You! Celia! Poppa, when he was sick. Everybody! . . . Don't you ask *me* "What people"! How many beatings from Momma did I get for things that you did? How many dresses did I go without so you could look like someone when you went out? I was the workhorse and you were the pretty one. You have no right to talk to me like that. No right.

BLANCHE   This is all about Jack, isn't it? You're blaming me for what happened.

KATE   Why do you think that man is sick today? Why did a policeman have to carry him home at two o'clock in the morning? So your Nora could have dancing lessons? So that Laurie could see a doctor every three weeks? Go on! Worry about your friend across the street, not the ones who have to be dragged home to keep a roof over your head.
   (She turns away. JACK *walks in from the kitchen)*

JACK   What is this? What's going on here?

BLANCHE *(To* KATE*)*   Why didn't you ever tell me you felt that way?

KATE (*Turns her back to her*) I never had the time. I was too busy taking care of everyone.

JACK What is it, Blanche? What happened?
(*She hands* JACK *the letter. He starts to read it*)

BLANCHE It took all these years? It took something like that letter for you to finally get your feelings out?

KATE I didn't need a letter . . . I just needed you to ask me.
(BLANCHE *is terribly hurt and extremely vulnerable standing there*)

BLANCHE Laurie! Please go upstairs. This conversation isn't for you.

EUGENE The ice cream is ready.

BLANCHE Eugene, put the ice cream in the icebox. I have to talk to your mother.
(EUGENE *goes into the kitchen*)

JACK (*Finishes the letter*) I never spoke to the woman. They've lived in that house for three years, and I never exchanged a word with her.

KATE (*To* JACK) What are you walking around for? If you're out of bed, at least sit in a chair.

BLANCHE If I could take Nora and Laurie and pack them out of this house tonight, I would do it. But I can't. I have no place to take them.

JACK Blanche! What are you talking about? Don't say such things.

BLANCHE (*Looks straight at* KATE)   If I can leave the girls with you for another few weeks, I would appreciate it. Until I can find a place of my own, and then I'll send for them.

JACK   You're not sending for anybody and you're not leaving anywhere. I don't want to hear this kind of talk.

KATE   Stay out of this, Jack. Let her do what she wants.

BLANCHE   I know a woman in Manhattan Beach. I can stay with her for a few days. And then I'll find a job. I will do *anything* anybody asks me, but I will *never* be a burden to anyone again.
    (*She starts for the stairs*)

JACK   Blanche, stop this! Stop it right now. What the hell is going on here, for God's sakes? Two sisters having a fight they should have had twenty-five years ago. You want to get it out, Blanche, get it out! Tell her what it's like to live in a house that isn't yours. To have to depend on somebody else to put the food on your plate every night. I know what it's like because I lived that way until I was twenty-one years old . . . Tell her, Kate, what it is to be an older sister. To suddenly be the one who has to work and shoulder all the responsibilities and not be the one who gets the affection and the hugs when you were the only one there. You think I don't see it with Stanley and Eugene? With Nora and Laurie? You think I don't hear the fights that go on up in those rooms night after night? Go on, Kate! Scream at her! Yell at her. Call her names, Blanche. Tell her to go to hell for the first time in your life . . . And when you both got it out of your systems, give each other a hug and go have dinner. My lousy ice cream is melting, for God's sakes.

(*There is a long silence*)

BLANCHE   I love you both very much. No matter what Kate says to me, I will never stop loving her. But I have to get out. If I don't do it now, I will lose whatever self-respect I have left. For people like us, sometimes the only thing we really own is our dignity . . . and when I grow old, I would like to have as much as Mrs. Matthew Murphy across the street.

(*She turns and goes up the stairs, disappearing into her room*)

JACK   What did it, Kate? Something terrible must have happened to you tonight for you to behave like this. It wasn't Blanche. It was something else. What was it, Kate?

KATE (*Stares out the window*)   Tell the kids to come down in five minutes. We're eating in the kitchen tonight.

(*She walks into the kitchen.* JACK *stands there, staring after her.* EUGENE, *coming out of the kitchen, passes his father*)

JACK   Get Stanley and Laurie. Dinner is in five minutes.

(JACK *goes into the kitchen.* EUGENE *walks to the stairs and up toward his bedroom*)

EUGENE (*To the audience*)   It was the first day in my life I didn't get blamed for what just happened. I felt real sorry for everybody, but as long as I wasn't to blame, I didn't feel all *that* bad about things. That's when I realized I had a selfish streak in me. I sure hope I grow out of it. *(He enters his bedroom and says to* STANLEY*)* Aunt Blanche is leaving.

STANLEY *(Sits up)* For where?

EUGENE *(Sits on his own bed)* To stay with some woman in Manhattan Beach. She and Mom just had a big fight. She's going to send for Laurie and Nora when she gets a job.

STANLEY What did they fight about?

EUGENE I couldn't hear it all. I think Mom sorta blames Aunt Blanche for Pop having to work so hard.

STANLEY *(Hits the pillow with his fist)* Oh, God! . . . Did Mom say anything about me? About how I lost my salary?

EUGENE You told her? Why did you tell her? I came up with twelve terrific lies for you.
        *(*STANLEY *opens his drawer, puts on a sweater)*

STANLEY How much money do you have?

EUGENE Me? I don't have any money.

STANLEY *(Puts another sweater over the first one)* The hell you don't. You've got money in your cigar box. How much do you have?

EUGENE I got a dollar twelve. It's my life's savings.

STANLEY Let me have it. I'll pay it back, don't worry.
        (He puts a jacket over the sweaters, then gets a fedora from the closet and puts it on. EUGENE *takes the cigar box from under the bed, opens it)*

EUGENE   What are you putting on all those things for?

STANLEY   In case I have to sleep out tonight. I'm leaving, Gene. I don't know where I'm going yet, but I'll write to you when I get there.

EUGENE   You're leaving home?

STANLEY   When I'm gone, you tell Aunt Blanche what happened to my salary. Then she'll know why Mom was so angry. Tell her please not to leave, because it was all my fault, not Mom's. Will you do that?
   (*He takes the coins out of the cigar box*)

EUGENE   I have eight cents' worth of stamps, if you want that too.

STANLEY   Thanks. (*He picks up a small medal*) What's this?

EUGENE   The medal you won for the hundred-yard dash two years ago.

STANLEY   From the Police Athletic League. I didn't know you still had this.

EUGENE   You gave it to me. You can have it back if you want it.

STANLEY   It's not worth anything.

EUGENE   It is to me.

STANLEY   Sure. You can keep it.

EUGENE   Thanks . . . Where will you go?

STANLEY   I don't know. I've been thinking about joining the Army. Pop says we'll be at war in a couple of years anyway. I could be a sergeant or something by the time it starts.

EUGENE   If it lasts long enough, I could join too. Maybe we can get in the same outfit. "The Fighting 69th." It's mostly Irish, but they had a few Jewish guys in the movie.

STANLEY   You don't go in the Army unless they come and get you. You go to college. You hear me? Promise me you'll go to college.

EUGENE   I'll probably have to stay home and work if you leave. We'll need the money.

STANLEY   I'll send home my paycheck every month. A sergeant in the Army makes real good dough . . . Well, I better get going.

EUGENE   (On the verge of tears)   What do you have to leave for?

STANLEY   Don't start crying. They'll hear you.

EUGENE   They'll get over it. They won't stay mad at you forever. I was mad at you and *I* got over it.

STANLEY   Because of me, the whole family is breaking up. Do you want Nora to end up like one of those cheap boardwalk girls?

EUGENE   I don't care. I'm not in love with Nora anymore.

STANLEY   Well, you *should* care. She's your cousin. Don't turn out to be like me.

EUGENE   I don't see what's so bad about you.

STANLEY (*Looks at him*) Take care of yourself, Eug. (*They embrace. He opens the door, looks around, then back to* EUGENE) If you ever write a story about me, call me Hank. I always liked the name Hank.
(*He goes, closing the door behind him.*

> EUGENE *sits there in silence for a while, then turns to the audience*)

EUGENE   I guess there comes a time in everybody's life when you say, "This very moment is the end of my childhood." When Stanley closed the door, I knew that moment had come to me . . . I was scared. I was lonely. And I hated my mother and father for making him so unhappy. Even if they were right, I still hated them . . . I even hated Stanley a little because he left me there to grow up all by myself.

KATE (*Yelling*) Eugene! Laurie! It's dinner. I'm not waiting all night.

EUGENE (*To the audience*)   And I hated her for leaving Stanley's name out when she called us for dinner. I don't think parents really know how cruel they can be sometimes . . . (*A beat*) At dinner I tried to tell them about Stanley, but I just couldn't get the words out . . . I left the table without even having my ice cream . . . If it was suffering I was after, I was beginning to learn about it.

> (KATE *and* JACK *come out of the kitchen, heading upstairs*)

JACK   It's ten o'clock, where is Stanley so late?

KATE   Never mind Stanley. You should have been in bed an hour ago.

JACK   Why won't you tell me what happened between you and that boy?

KATE   I'm tired, Jack. I've had enough to deal with for one day.

JACK   I want him to go to temple with me on Saturday. They stop going for three or four weeks, they forget their religion altogether.
(They go into the bedroom)

EUGENE   The house became quieter than I ever heard it before. Aunt Blanche was in her room packing, Pop and Mom were in their bedroom, and I had to talk to somebody or else I'd go crazy. I didn't have much choice. *(He walks over to her room and knocks on the door)* Laurie? It's Eugene. Can I come in?

LAURIE   What do you want? I'm reading.

EUGENE   *(Opens the door)*   I just want to talk to you.

LAURIE   I didn't say yes, did I?

EUGENE   Well, I'm already in, so it's too late . . . What are you reading?

LAURIE   *The Citadel* by A. J. Cronin.

EUGENE   I read it. It's terrific . . . I hear your mother's leaving in the morning.

LAURIE   We're going too as soon as she finds a job.

EUGENE   I can't believe it. I'm going to be the only one left here.

LAURIE   You mean you and Stanley.

EUGENE   Stanley's gone. He's not coming back. I think he's going to join the Army.

LAURIE   You mean he ran away?

EUGENE   No. Only kids run away. When you're Stanley's age, you just leave.

LAURIE   He didn't say goodbye?

EUGENE   My parents don't even know about it. I'm going to tell them now.

LAURIE   I wonder if I'll have to go to a different school.

EUGENE   You'll have to make all new friends.

LAURIE   I don't care. I don't have any friends here anyway.

EUGENE   Because you're always in the house. You never go out.

LAURIE   I can't because of my condition.

EUGENE   You don't look sick to me. Do you *feel* sick?

LAURIE   No. But my mother tells me I am.

EUGENE   I don't trust parents anymore.

LAURIE   Why would she lie to me?

EUGENE   To keep you around. Once they find out Stanley's gone, they're going to handcuff me to my bed.

LAURIE   I wouldn't leave my mother anyway. Even when I'm older. Even if I get married. I'll never leave my mother.

EUGENE   Yeah? Mr. Murphy across the street never left his mother. And he ended up going to jail.

LAURIE   None of this would have happened if my father was alive.

EUGENE   How did you feel when he died?

LAURIE   I don't remember. I cried a lot because I saw my mother crying.

EUGENE   I would hate it if my father died. Especially with Stanley gone. We'd probably have to move out of this house.

LAURIE   Well . . . then you and your mother could come and live with us.

EUGENE   So if we all end up living together, what's the point in breaking up now?

LAURIE   I don't know. I have to finish reading.
        (She goes back to her book. EUGENE gets up and looks at the audience)

EUGENE   You don't get too far talking to Laurie. Sometimes I think the flutter in her heart is really in her brain. (He leaves the room, closes the door and heads down the stairs) I went into their bedroom and broke the news about Stanley. The monumental news that their eldest son had run off, probably to get killed in France fighting for his country. My mother said, "Go to bed. He'll be home when it gets cold out." I couldn't believe

it. Their own son. It was then that I suspected that Stanley and I were adopted . . . They finally went to bed and I waited out on the front steps until it got cold, but Stanley never showed up.
(*He goes out the front door.*

It is later that night, after midnight. We see NORA *enter the front yard.* BLANCHE *comes down the stairs in a nightgown and a robe. She waits at the foot of the stairs as* NORA *comes into the house and sees her*)

BLANCHE   I wanted to talk to you.

NORA   Now? It's late.

BLANCHE   I know it's late. We could have talked earlier if you didn't come home at twelve o'clock at night.
(BLANCHE *walks into the living room.* NORA *follows her in and stands in the doorway*)

NORA   How was your dinner?

BLANCHE   I didn't go. Mr. Murphy was in an accident.

NORA   I'm sorry. Is he all right?

BLANCHE   He's got his problems, like the rest of us . . . I was very hurt that you left tonight without saying goodbye.

NORA   I was late. Someone was waiting for me.

BLANCHE   So was I. You knew it was important to me.

NORA   I'm not feeling very well.

BLANCHE   You purposely left without seeing me. You've never done that before.

NORA   Can we talk about this in the morning?

BLANCHE   I won't be here in the morning.

NORA   Then tomorrow night.

BLANCHE   I'm leaving, Nora. I'm moving out in the morning.

NORA   What are you talking about?

BLANCHE   Aunt Kate and I had a fight tonight. We said some terrible things to each other. Things that have been bottled up since we were children. I'm going to stay with my friend Louise in Manhattan Beach until I can find a job. Then I'll send for you and Laurie.

NORA   I can't believe it. You mean it's all right for you to leave *us* but it wasn't all right for me to leave *you*?

BLANCHE   I was never concerned about your leaving *me*. It was your future I was worrying about.

NORA   It was *my* future. Why couldn't *I* have something to say about it?

BLANCHE   Maybe I was wrong, I don't know. I never made the decisions for the family. Your father did. Aunt Kate was right about one thing: everyone always took care of me. My mother, my sisters, your father, even you and Laurie. I've been a very dependent person all my life.

NORA   Maybe that's all I'm asking for. To be *in*dependent.

BLANCHE *(Sternly)*   You *earn* your independence. You don't take it at the expense of others. Would that job even be offered to you if somebody in this family hadn't paid for those dancing lessons and kept a roof over your head and clothes on your back? If anyone's going to pay back Uncle Jack, it'll be me—doing God knows what, I don't know—but one thing I'm sure of. I'll *steal* before I let my daughter show that man one ounce of ingratitude or disrespect.

NORA   So I have to give up the one chance I may never get again, is that it? I'm the one who has to pay for what you couldn't do with your own life.

BLANCHE *(Angrily)*   What right do you have to judge me like that?

NORA   *Judge* you? I can't even talk to you. I don't exist to you. I have tried so hard to get close to you but there was never any room. Whatever you had to give went to Daddy, and when he died, whatever was left you gave to—
(*She turns away*)

BLANCHE   What? Finish what you were going to say.

NORA   . . . I have been jealous my whole life of Laurie because she was lucky enough to be born sick. I could never turn a light on in my room at night or read in bed because Laurie always needed her precious sleep. I could never have a friend over on the weekends because Laurie was always resting. I used to pray I'd get

some terrible disease or get hit by a car so I'd have a leg all twisted or crippled and then once, maybe just once, *I'd* get to crawl into bed next to you on a cold rainy night and talk to you and hold you until I fell asleep in your arms . . . just once . . .
(*She is in tears*)

BLANCHE   My God, Nora . . . is that what you think of me?

NORA   Is it any worse than what you think of me?

BLANCHE (*Hesitates, trying to recover*)   I'm not going to let you hurt me, Nora. I'm not going to let you tell me that I don't love you or that I haven't tried to give you as much as I gave Laurie . . . God knows I'm not perfect, because enough angry people in this house told me so tonight. But I am *not* going to be a doormat for all the frustrations and unhappiness that you or Aunt Kate or anyone else wants to lay at my feet . . . I did *not* create this universe. I do *not* decide who lives and dies, or who's rich or poor or who feels loved and who feels deprived. If you feel cheated that Laurie gets more than you, then I feel cheated that I had a husband who died at thirty-six. And if you keep on feeling that way, you'll end up like me—with something much worse than loneliness or helplessness and that's self-pity. Believe me, there is no leg that's twisted or bent that is more crippling than a human being who thrives on his own misfortunes . . . I am sorry, Nora, that you feel unloved and I will do everything I can to change it except apologize for it. I am *tired* of apologizing. After a while it becomes your life's work and it doesn't bring any money into the house. If it's taken your pain and

Aunt Kate's anger to get me to start living again, then God will give me the strength to make it up to you, but I will *not* go back to being that frightened, helpless woman that *I* created! I've already buried someone I love. Now it's time to bury someone I hate.

NORA   I didn't ask you to hate yourself. I just asked you to love me.

BLANCHE   I do, Nora. Oh, God, why can't I make that clear to you?

NORA   I feel so terrible.

BLANCHE   Why?

NORA   Because I think I hurt you and I still want that job with Mr. Beckman.

BLANCHE   I know you do.

NORA   But I can't have it, can I?

BLANCHE   How can I answer that without you thinking I'm still depriving you?

NORA   I don't know . . . Maybe you just did.

BLANCHE   I hope so, Nora. I pray to God it's so.
        (KATE *is coming down the stairs*)

KATE   I heard voices downstairs. I didn't know who it was.

BLANCHE   I'm sorry if we woke you . . . Go on up to bed, Nora. We'll talk again in the morning.

NORA   All right . . . Good night, Aunt Kate.
        (NORA *goes upstairs*)

KATE   Is she all right?

BLANCHE   Yes.

KATE   She's not angry anymore?

BLANCHE   No, Kate. No one's angry anymore. (NORA *goes into the bedroom*) I just explained everything to Nora. The girls will help you with all the housework while I'm gone. Laurie's strong enough to do her share. I've kept her being a baby long enough.

KATE   They've never been any trouble to me, those girls. Never.

BLANCHE   I'll try to take them on the weekends if I can . . . It's late. We could both use a good night's sleep.
    (*She starts out of the room*)

KATE   Blanche! Don't go! (BLANCHE *stops*) I feel badly enough for what I said. Don't make me feel any worse.

BLANCHE   Everything you said to me tonight was true, Kate. I wish to God you'd said it years ago.

KATE   What would I do without you? Who else do I have to talk to all day? What friends do I have in this neighborhood? Even the Murphys across the street are leaving.

BLANCHE   You and I never had any troubles before to-night, Kate. And as God is in heaven, there'll never be an angry word between us again . . . It's the girls I'm thinking of now. We have to be together. The three of us. It's what they want as much as I do.

KATE   All right. I'm not saying you shouldn't have it. But you're not going to find a job overnight. Apartments are expensive. While you're looking, why do you have to live with strangers in Manhattan Beach?

BLANCHE   Louise isn't a stranger. She's a good friend.

KATE   To me good friends are strangers. But sisters are sisters.

BLANCHE   I'm afraid of becoming comfortable here. If I don't get out now, when will I ever do it?

KATE   The door is open. Go whenever you want. When you got the job, when you find the apartment, I'll help you move. I can look with you. I know how to bargain with these landlords.

BLANCHE *(Smiles)*   You wouldn't mind doing that?

KATE   They see a woman all alone, they take advantage of you . . . I'll find out what they're asking for the Murphy place. It couldn't be expensive, she never cleaned it.

BLANCHE   How independent can I become if I live right across the street from you?

KATE   Far enough away for you to close your own door, and close enough for me not to feel so lonely.
   (BLANCHE *looks at her with great affection, walks over to* KATE *and embraces her. They hold on dearly*)

BLANCHE   If I lived on the moon, you would still be close to me, Kate.

KATE   I'll tell Jack. He wouldn't go to sleep until I promised to come up with some good news.

BLANCHE   I suddenly feel so hungry.

KATE   Of course. You haven't had dinner. Come on. I'll fix you some scrambled eggs.
(She heads toward the kitchen)

BLANCHE   I'll make them. I'm an independent woman now.

KATE   With your eyes, you'll never get the eggs in the pan.
(They walk into the kitchen.
EUGENE *appears in the front yard. He is carrying two bags of groceries. It is late afternoon. He stops to talk to the audience)*

EUGENE   So Aunt Blanche decided to stay while she was looking for a job. Nora went back to school the next morning, gave me a big smile and her legs looked as creamy-white as ever. Laurie was asked to take out the garbage but she quickly got a "flutter" in her heart, so I had to do it. Life was back to normal.
(He goes into the house. KATE *comes out of the kitchen)*

KATE   Eugene! Go back to Greenblatt's. I need flour.

EUGENE   How much? A teaspoonful? *(She glares at him, takes the bags and goes back into the kitchen. He turns to the audience)* Stanley didn't come home that night, and even though Mom didn't say anything, I knew she was plenty worried. She told Pop how Stanley lost the money playing poker, and from the sounds coming out of their room, I figured Stanley should forget about the Army and try for the Foreign Legion. (STANLEY *appears down the street*) And then all of a sudden, the next night about dinnertime, he came back. I was never so happy to see anyone in my whole life.

STANLEY   Hi! *(He looks around)* Where's Mom and Pop?

EUGENE   Mom's in the kitchen cooking. Pop's upstairs with his prayer book. They figured if God didn't bring you home, maybe her potato pancakes would . . . What happened? Did you join up?

STANLEY   I came pretty close. I passed the physical one two three.

EUGENE   I knew you would.

STANLEY   They were giving me cigarettes, doughnuts, the whole sales pitch. I mean, they really wanted me.

EUGENE   I'll bet.

STANLEY   But then, just as I was about to sign my name, I stopped cold. I put down the pen and said, "I'm sorry. Maybe some other time"—and walked out.

EUGENE   How come?

STANLEY   I couldn't do it to Pop. Right now he needs me more than the Army does . . . I knew Mom didn't really mean it when she said she'd never forgive me for losing the money, but if I walked out on the family now, maybe she never would.

EUGENE   Gee, I thought you'd be halfway to training camp by now . . . but I'm real glad you're home, Stan.
(*They stand there looking at each other for a moment as* KATE *walks out of the kitchen to the yard*)

KATE   Eugene. I need a pint of sweet cream. And some more sugar.

EUGENE   Stanley's home.

STANLEY   Hello, Mom.

KATE (*Looks at him, then to* EUGENE)   Get a two-pound bag. I want to bake a chocolate cake.

EUGENE   A two-pound bag from Greenblatt's? I'll need identification.
(*He looks at* STANLEY, *then goes*)

KATE (*To* STANLEY)   Are you staying for dinner?

STANLEY   I'm staying as long as you'll let me stay.

KATE   Why wouldn't I let you stay?? This is your home.
(KATE *walks into the house,* STANLEY *follows.* JACK *comes down the stairs and goes over to his favorite chair. He opens up his paper*) Your father's been very worried. I think you owe him some sort of explanation.

STANLEY   I was just about to do that. (KATE *looks at him, wants to reach out to touch him, but can't seem to do it. She goes back into the kitchen as* STANLEY *walks into the living room*) Hi, Pop. How you feeling? (JACK *doesn't turn. He keeps reading his newspaper*) I'm sorry about not coming home last night . . . I know it was wrong. I just didn't know how to tell you about the

money. I know it doesn't help to say I'll never do it again, because I won't. I swear. Never . . . *(He takes money out of his pocket)* I've got three dollars. Last night I went over to Dominick's Bowling Alley and I set pins till midnight and I could make another six on the weekend, so that makes nine. I'll get the seventeen dollars back, Pop, I promise . . . I'm not afraid of hard work. That's the one thing you taught me. Hard work and principles. That's the code I'm going to live by for the rest of my life . . . So—if you have anything you want to say to me, I'd be very glad to listen.
    (He stands there and waits)

JACK *(Still looking at the paper)* Did you read the paper tonight, Stanley?

STANLEY No, Pop.

JACK There's going to be a war. A terrible war, Stanley.

STANLEY I know, Pop.
    (He moves into the room, faces his father)

JACK The biggest war the world has ever seen. And it frightens me. We're still not over the last one yet, and already they're starting another one.

STANLEY We don't talk about it much in the store because of Mr. Stroheim being German and all.

JACK My brother, Michael, was killed in the last war. I've told you that.

STANLEY You showed me his picture in uniform.

JACK   He was nineteen years old. The day he left, he
   didn't look any older than Eugene. He was killed the
   second week he was overseas . . .

STANLEY   I know.

JACK   They didn't take me because I was sixteen years
   old, both parents were dead, and I lived with my Aunt
   Rose and Uncle Maury. They had two sons in the
   Navy, both of them wounded, both of them decorated.

STANLEY   Uncle Leon and Uncle Paul, right?

JACK (*Nods*)   My brother would have been forty years
   old this month. He was a handsome boy. Good athlete,
   good dancer, good everything. I idolized him. Like
   Eugene idolizes you.

STANLEY   No, he doesn't.

JACK   He does, believe me. I hear him outside, talking to
   his friends. "My brother this, my brother that" . . .
   Brothers can talk to each other the way fathers and sons
   never do . . . I never knew a thing about girls until my
   brother taught me. Isn't it like that with you and Eugene?

STANLEY   Yeah, I tell him a few things.

JACK   That's good. I'm glad you're so close . . . I missed
   all that when Michael went away. That's why I'm glad
   you didn't do anything foolish last night. I was afraid
   maybe you'd run away. I hear you talking with Eugene
   sometimes about the Army. That day will come soon
   enough, I'm afraid.

STANLEY   I did think about it. It was on my mind.

JACK   Don't you know, Stanley, there's nothing you could ever do that was so terrible, I couldn't forgive you. I know why you gambled. I know how terrible you feel. It was foolish, you know that already. I've lost money gambling in my time, I know what it's like.

STANLEY   You did?

JACK   You're so surprised? You think your father's a perfect human being? Someday I'll tell you some other things I did that wasn't so perfect. Not even your mother knows. If you grow up thinking I was perfect, you'll hate yourself for every mistake you ever make. Don't be so hard on yourself. That's what you've got a mother and father to do.

STANLEY   You're not hard on me. You're always fair.

JACK   I try to be. You're a good son, Stanley. You don't even realize that. We have men in our cutting room who haven't spoken to their sons in five, six years. Boys who have no respect for anyone, including themselves; who haven't worked a day in their lives, or who've brought their parents a single day's pleasure. Thank God, I could never say that about you, Stanley.

STANLEY   I gambled away seventeen dollars and you're telling me how terrific I am.

JACK   Hey, wait a minute. Don't get the wrong idea. If you were home last night when your mother told me, I would have thrown you and your clothes out the window. Today I'm calmer. Today I read the newspaper. Today I'm afraid for all of us.

STANLEY I understand.

JACK After dinner tonight, you apologize to your mother and give her the three dollars.

STANLEY I will.

JACK And apologize to your Aunt Blanche because she was worried about you too.

STANLEY I will.

JACK And you can thank your brother as well. He came into my bedroom this afternoon and told me how badly you felt. He was almost in tears himself. The way he pleaded your case, I thought I had Clarence Darrow in the room.

STANLEY Eugene's a terrific kid.

JACK All right. Go wash up and get ready for dinner. And tonight, you and I are going to go out in the backyard and I'm going to teach you how to play poker.

STANLEY *(Smiles)* Terrific!
      (He turns to go when KATE *comes out of the kitchen)*

KATE Is Eugene back yet?

STANLEY No, Mom.

KATE You look tired. Did you get any sleep?

STANLEY I got enough. I slept at a friend's house. Can I talk to you after dinner, Mom?

KATE Where am I going? To a night club?

STANLEY I'll wash up and be right down.
(*He turns and starts up the stairs*)

KATE Stanley! You didn't join anything, did you?

STANLEY No, Mom.

KATE You've got time yet. The family's growing up fast enough.

STANLEY Yes, Mom.
(*He turns and rushes up the stairs.* KATE *turns and looks at* JACK)

JACK It's all right. Everything is all right.

KATE Who said it wasn't? Didn't I say he'd be home? (*She calls up*) Laurie! Call your sister. Time to set the table.
(EUGENE *comes running into the house with a small bag and some letters*)

EUGENE (*Out of breath*) I just broke the world's record to Greenblatt's. Next year I'm entering the Grocery Store Olympics. Here's some mail for you, Pop.

KATE Is that my sweet cream?

EUGENE Never spilled a drop. The perfect run. (*She takes the bag and goes into the kitchen*) Where's Stanley?

JACK (*Takes the mail*) He's cleaning up. (*He looks at the mail*) Oh, my God, I've got jury duty next week.
(*He sits and opens up a letter.* EUGENE *rushes up the stairs and runs into his room.* STANLEY *is taking off his two sweaters*)

EUGENE (*Closing the door*) Are you back in the family?

STANLEY Yeah. Everything's great.

EUGENE Terrific . . . You want to take a walk on the boardwalk tonight? See what's doing?

STANLEY I can't tonight. I'm busy.

EUGENE Doing what?

STANLEY I'm playing poker.

EUGENE Poker? Are you serious?

STANLEY Yeah. Right after dinner.

EUGENE I don't believe you.

STANLEY I swear to God! I got a poker game tonight.

EUGENE You're crazy! You're genuinely crazy, Stanley . . . If you lose, I'm not sticking up for you this time.

STANLEY If you don't tell anybody, I'll give you a present.

EUGENE What kind of present?

STANLEY Are you going to tell?

EUGENE No. What's my present?
(STANLEY *takes something wrapped in a piece of paper out of his jacket and hands it to* EUGENE)

STANLEY Here. It's for you. Don't leave it lying around the room.
(EUGENE *starts to open it. It's postcard size*)

EUGENE   What is it?

STANLEY   Open it slowly. (EUGENE *does*) Slower than that . . . Close your eyes. (EUGENE *does. It is unwrapped*) Now look!
(EUGENE *looks. His eyes almost pop out*)

EUGENE   OH, MY GOD!! . . . SHE'S NAKED! YOU CAN SEE *EVERYTHING*!!

STANLEY   Lower your voice. You want to get caught with a thing like that?

EUGENE   Where did you get it? Who is she?

STANLEY   She's French. That's how *all* the women are in Paris.

EUGENE   I can't believe I'm looking at this? You mean some girl actually *posed* for this? She just lay there and let some guy take a picture?
(BLANCHE *comes out of the kitchen*)

BLANCHE   Laurie! Nora! Time for dinner.
(*The girls come out of their room*)

STANLEY   It belongs to the guy who owes me two and a half bucks. I can keep it until he pays me back.

EUGENE   Don't take the money. Let him keep it for a while.
(*He lies back on the bed, staring at the picture.*
NORA *and* LAURIE *go down the stairs as* KATE *comes out of the kitchen with plates and starts to set up the table*)

STANLEY   That's my appreciation for being a good buddy.

EUGENE   Anytime you need a favor, just let me know.

STANLEY   Put it in a safe spot . . . Come on. It's dinner.

EUGENE   In a minute. I'll be down in a minute.
(*He lies there, eyes transfixed.* STANLEY *starts down the stairs.* NORA *and* LAURIE *set out napkins and utensils.* BLANCHE *starts to arrange the chairs.*

JACK, *with a letter in his hand, gets up, looking excited, walks into the dining room*)

JACK   Kate? Where's Kate?

KATE   Don't run. You're always running.

JACK (*Holds up the letter*)   It's a letter from London. My cousin Sholem got out. They got out of Poland. They're free, Kate!

BLANCHE   Thank God!

JACK   His wife, his mother, all four children. They're sailing for New York tomorrow. They'll be here in a week.

KATE   In a week?

LAURIE   Do they speak English?

JACK   I don't think so. A few words, maybe. (*To* KATE) They had to sell everything. They took only what they could carry.

STANLEY   Where will they stay?

JACK   Well, I'll have to discuss it with the family. Some with Uncle Leon, Uncle Paul—

KATE   With us. We can put some beds in the dining room. It's easier to eat in the kitchen anyway.

BLANCHE   The little ones can stay with Laurie. Nora can sleep with me—can't you, dear?

NORA (*Pleased*)   Of course, Momma.

STANLEY   Don't worry about money, Pa. I'm going to hit Mr. Stroheim for that raise.

JACK   They got out. That's all that's important. They got out.

(JACK *sits down at the table to reread the letter.* NORA, STANLEY *and* LAURIE *look over his shoulder.* BLANCHE *and* KATE *set the table*)

KATE (*Yells up*)   Eugene! We're all waiting for you!

EUGENE (*Calls down*)   Be right there! I just have to write down something. (*He looks at photo again, then picks up fountain pen and his memoir book and reads as he begins to write*) "October the second, six twenty-five P.M. A momentous moment in the life of I, Eugene Morris Jerome. I have seen the Golden Palace of the Himalayas . . . Puberty is over. Onward and upwards!"
                              Curtain

Since 1960, a Broadway season without a Neil Simon comedy or musical has been a rare one. His first play was *Come Blow Your Horn*, followed by the musical *Little Me*. During the 1966–67 season, *Barefoot in the Park*, *The Odd Couple*, *Sweet Charity* and *The Star-Spangled Girl* were all running simultaneously; in the 1970–71 season, Broadway theatergoers had their choice of *Plaza Suite*, *Last of the Red Hot Lovers* and *Promises, Promises*. Next came *The Gingerbread Lady*, *The Prisoner of Second Avenue*, *The Sunshine Boys*, *The Good Doctor*, *God's Favorite*, *California Suite*, *Chapter Two*, *They're Playing Our Song*, *I Ought to Be in Pictures*, *Fools*, and most recently, a revival of *Little Me*.

NEIL SIMON began his writing career in television, writing *The Phil Silvers Show* and Sid Caesar's *Your Show of Shows*. Mr. Simon has also written for the screen: the adaptations of *Barefoot in the Park*, *The Odd Couple*, *Plaza Suite*, *The Prisoner of Second Avenue*, *The Sunshine Boys*, *California Suite*, *Chapter Two*, and most recently, *I Ought to Be in Pictures*. His other screenplays include *The Out-of-Towners*, *The Heartbreak Kid*, *Murder by Death*, *The Goodbye Girl*, *The Cheap Detective*, *Seems Like Old Times*, *Only When I Laugh* and *Max Dugan Returns*.

The author lives in California and New York. He has two daughters, Ellen and Nancy.

Ⓟ PLUME

CONTEMPORARY DRAMA

☐ **MOLLY SWEENEY by Brian Friel.** Molly herself, blind since she was an infant, tells of her world before and after an operation to try to restore her sight. Her husband, itinerant champion of good causes, talks of his passion to help her. Her once famous eye surgeon, now a whiskey-sodden recluse in Donegal, sees the operation as his chance to reclaim his reputation. Each of their voices interweaves, threading in and out with details, and carrying us effortlessly to an unexpected and poignant conclusion. "An entrancing drama. Rich with rapturous poetry."—David Richards, *New York Times*
(275083—$9.95)

☐ **FALSETTOS by William Finn and James Lapine.** This exuberant, Tony Award winning trilogy and Broadway smash traces the confusions, obsessions, loves and losses of Marvin on his journey of self-discovery. Captivating, imaginative, and powerful, this bittersweet musical portrays gay love and the complexities of modern relationships. "The richest emotional experience offered by any musical on Broadway."—*Time*
(270723—$11.00)

☐ **TWO TRAINS RUNNING a play by August Wilson.** With compassion, humor, and a superb sense of place and time, Wilson paints a vivid portrait of everyday lives in the shadow of great events, and of unsung men and women who are anything but ordinary. "A symphonic composition with a rich lode of humanity running through it."—*Los Angeles Times*
(269296—$8.00)

☐ **LOST IN YONKERS by Neil Simon.** What happens to children in the absence of love? That is the question that lies at the heart of this funny and heartrending play filled with laughter, tears and insight. "Neil Simon has done it again, with a craftsmanship and skill probably unmatched in the contemporary English-speaking theater."—Clive Barnes, *New York Post*
(268834—$8.00)

Prices slightly higher in Canada.